CUPCAKE
Party

A READER'S DIGEST BOOK
This edition published by
The Reader's Digest Association, Inc.
by arrangement with McRae Publishing Ltd

Copyright @ 2012 by McRae Publishing Ltd

Publishers: Anne McRae, Marco Nardi
Project Director Anne McRae
Art Director Marco Nardi
Photography Brent Parker Jones
Text Carla Bardi, Rachael Lane
Editing Foreign Concept
Food Styling Mark Hockenhull
Cupcake Designs Khistina Mulyomo, Emma Mackay
Layouts Aurora Granata
Prepress Filippo Delle Monache

ISBN 978-1-55475-128-0

For more Reader's Digest products and information,
visit our website: www.readersdigest.com.au

Printed in China

NOTE TO OUR READERS
Eating eggs or egg whites that are not completely
cooked poses the possibility of salmonella food
poisoning. The risk is greater for pregnant
women, the elderly, the very young, and
persons with impaired immune systems. If
you are concerned about salmonella,
you can use reconstituted powdered
egg whites or pasteurized eggs.

Carla Bardi, Rachael Lane

CUPCAKE

Party

Reader's
Digest

THE READER'S DIGEST ASSOCIATION, INC.
New York, New York / Montreal / Singapore

BAKER'S TIPS

This book is a celebration of cupcakes, of how simple they are to bake, and what fun they are to serve and eat. Here you will find 60 superb recipes, each one carefully explained and placed right next to a stunning photograph of a plate brimming with the finished cupcakes, showing you exactly how they will look. This book is a visual feast!

One of the great things about cupcakes is that they are so easy to make. Just a few ingredients (usually butter, sugar, eggs, and flour), flavored, beaten, and baked, are all that is required. The trick lies in preparing the pretty decorations. There are just a few basic rules:

BAKING: Cupcakes are quicker and simpler to bake than full-size cakes. Follow the recipes carefully and they will rise and turn golden without much effort on your part.

BUTTER: Make sure it is fresh; butter keeps in the refrigerator for 2–3 weeks only. Always use softened butter at room temperature when creaming with sugar. Beat by hand or in an electric mixer until pale and creamy. For baking, most brands of butter are fine, but for frostings, always use the highest quality available.

COCOA POWDER: Almost always needs sifting, to remove the lumps rather than to add air.

DECORATION: The key to cupcake joy lies in perfecting the frostings and toppings. Decorating a cupcake is not as difficult as decorating a full-size cake, plus you have at least 12 little cakes to practise on! Follow the instructions carefully in each recipe, and look closely at the detailed photographs on each page. This book will help you make some stunning cupcakes.

EGGS: Always use fresh eggs. Store them on the top shelf of the refrigerator rather than in the egg compartment on the door (which is not cool enough). Keep them in their cardboard carton; this will stop them from absorbing odors from other foods. Eggs come in different sizes; in these recipes we have used large, 2-ounce (60-g) eggs. When baking, eggs should be at room temperature; take them out of the refrigerator 1–2 hours before you start.

FLOUR: Modern flour is all pre-sifted, but we prefer to sift it again before adding to the batter.

PAPER LINERS: These are available in supermarkets and kitchen supply stores. Always line your pans with liners as this makes it easier to remove the cupcakes. Choose pretty, brightly-colored liners that suit the theme of your cupcakes. If liked, you can bake the cupcakes in plain liners, then remove and replace them with clean and bright new paper liners before frosting and serving.

SUGAR: Sugar is a basic ingredient in almost all cupcake recipes, adding both structure and texture to the finished product. Most of our recipes call for ordinary granulated sugar; a few make use of superfine (caster) sugar. If you don't have superfine sugar on hand you can make it easily by processing granulated sugar for 20–30 seconds in a food processor. Some recipes use light or dark brown sugar, which are readily available at the supermarket.

RAISING AGENTS: Most cupcake recipes include chemical raising agents, such as baking powder, or baking soda (bicarbonate of soda). Sometimes we have suggested that you use self-rising flour.

Cupcakes are usually baked in muffin pans. These pans are made of metal, silicone, or stoneware, and are lined with paper liners before adding the batter. A standard muffin cup is about 3 inches (75 mm) across and holds about 4 ounces (120 g) of batter. On these two pages we have visualized the basic steps for making cupcakes, from preparing the pans to cooling the freshly baked cupcakes.

CUPCAKE BASICS

1. Line a muffin pan with paper liners. Preheat the oven to the temperature indicated in each recipe. Remember that it will take 10–15 minutes for the oven to reach the desired temperature.

2. Before you begin mixing, set out all the ingredients listed in the recipe. Sift the flour and any other dry ingredients indicated in the recipe into a bowl and set aside, ready to add when you need them.

3. Most cupcakes are based on a mixture of butter and sugar, which is beaten until pale and creamy. If beating by hand, use a wooden spoon and beat vigorously for several minutes.

4. If you have an electric mixer, beat the butter and sugar on medium-high speed until pale and creamy.

5. Add the eggs one at a time, beating until just combined after each addition.

6. Beat in the flour mixture and any liquids listed in the recipe with the mixer on low speed, or with a wooden spoon.

7. Use a tablespoon to fill the paper liners two-thirds full with batter. Place in the preheated oven and bake for the time indicated in each recipe.

8. When cooked, the cupcakes should be risen and golden brown. Test by sticking a toothpick into the center. If it comes out clean, then the cupcakes are ready.

9. Place the muffin pan on a wire rack and let cool completely before removing the cupcakes from the pan.

grated...

TOPPING ½ cup (12...

Fresh blueberries, to dec...

MAKES 12 CUPCAKES • PREPARATIO...

BLUEBERRY CUP...

...ven to 350°F

...muffin

3. Bake fo...
golden brow...
inserted into the ce...
clean. Transfer the muffi...
wire rack. Let cool completely b...
removing the cupcakes.

TOPPING 4. Mix the yogurt and honey in a
small bowl. Top each cupcake with a dollop
of sweetened yogurt and a few fresh
blueberries. Decorate the cupcakes with
candy flowers, if liked. Serve at once.

CUPCAKES ON PAGE 96.

BUTTERFLY CUPCAKES

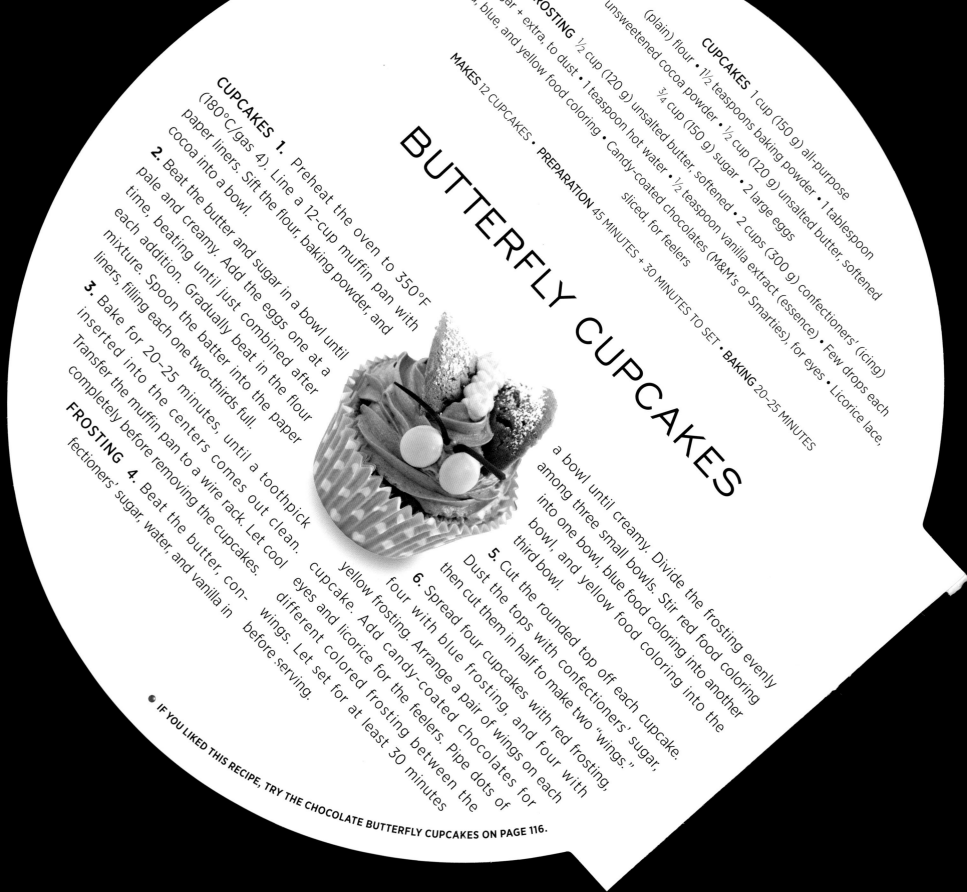

CUPCAKES 1 cup (150 g) all-purpose (plain) flour • 1½ teaspoons baking powder • 1 tablespoon unsweetened cocoa powder • ½ cup (120 g) unsalted butter, softened • ¾ cup (150 g) sugar • 2 large eggs • ½ teaspoon vanilla extract (essence) • Few drops each **FROSTING** ½ cup (120 g) unsalted butter, softened • 2 cups (300 g) confectioners' (icing) sugar + extra, to dust • 1 teaspoon hot water • Candy-coated chocolates (M&M's or Smarties), for eyes • Licorice lace, blue, and yellow food coloring • sliced, for feelers

MAKES 12 CUPCAKES • **PREPARATION** 45 MINUTES + 30 MINUTES TO SET • **BAKING** 20–25 MINUTES

CUPCAKES 1. Preheat the oven to 350°F (180°C/gas 4). Line a 12-cup muffin pan with paper liners. Sift the flour, baking powder, and cocoa into a bowl.
2. Beat the butter and sugar in a bowl until pale and creamy. Add the eggs one at a time, beating until just combined after each addition. Gradually beat in the flour mixture. Spoon the batter into the paper liners, filling each one two-thirds full.
3. Bake for 20–25 minutes, until a toothpick inserted into the centers comes out clean. Transfer the muffin pan to a wire rack. Let cool completely before removing the cupcakes.
FROSTING 4. Beat the butter, confectioners' sugar, water, and vanilla in

a bowl until creamy. Divide the frosting evenly among three small bowls. Stir red food coloring into one bowl, blue food coloring into another bowl, and yellow food coloring into the third bowl.
5. Cut the rounded top off each cupcake. Dust the tops with confectioners' sugar, then cut them in half to make two "wings."
6. Spread four cupcakes with red frosting, four with blue frosting, and four with yellow frosting. Arrange a pair of wings on each cupcake. Add candy-coated chocolates for eyes and licorice for the feelers. Pipe dots of different colored frosting between the wings. Let set for at least 30 minutes before serving.

IF YOU LIKED THIS RECIPE, TRY THE CHOCOLATE BUTTERFLY CUPCAKES ON PAGE 116.

VANILLA CUPCAKE PARTY

CUPCAKES 1⅓ cups (200 g) all-purpose (plain) flour • 1 teaspoon baking powder • ⅛ teaspoon salt • ¾ cup (180 g) unsalted butter • ¾ cup (180 g) sugar • ½ vanilla pod • 3 large eggs

BUTTERCREAM ½ cup (120 g) unsalted butter • 3 cups (450 g) confectioners' (icing) sugar • 1 tablespoon milk • 1 teaspoon vanilla extract (essence) • Few drops pink food coloring • Colored candy flowers, to decorate • Colored sugar, to sprinkle

MAKES 12 CUPCAKES • **PREPARATION** 30 MINUTES + 30 MINUTES TO SET • **BAKING** 20-25 MINUTES

CUPCAKES 1. Preheat the oven to 350°F (180°C/gas 4). Line a 12-cup muffin pan with paper liners. Sift the flour, baking powder, and salt into a bowl.

2. Beat the butter and sugar in a bowl until pale and creamy. Split the vanilla pod in half and scrape the seeds into the bowl. Add the eggs one at a time, beating until just combined after each addition. Beat in the flour mixture until just combined. Spoon the batter into the paper liners, filling each one two-thirds full.

3. Bake for 20-25 minutes, until a toothpick inserted into the centers comes out clean. Transfer the muffin pan to a wire rack. Let cool completely before removing the cupcakes.

BUTTERCREAM 4. Beat the butter, confectioners' sugar, milk, and vanilla in a bowl until pale and smooth. Divide the buttercream evenly between two bowls. Tint one bowl with pink food coloring.

5. Spoon the pink buttercream into a pastry (piping) bag. Pipe over half the cupcakes. Clean the pastry bag and fill with the plain buttercream. Pipe over the remaining cupcakes. Decorate each cupcake differently using the candy flowers and colored sugar. Let set for 30 minutes before serving.

● **IF YOU LIKED THIS RECIPE, TRY THE ROSY CUPCAKES ON PAGE 18.**

CUPCAKES 1½ cups (225 g) all-purpose
(plain) flour • 1 teaspoon baking powder • ⅛ teaspoon salt
½ cup (120 g) unsalted butter, softened • ¾ cup (150 g) sugar • 1 teaspoon
vanilla extract (essence) • 2 large eggs • ½ cup (120 ml) milk
RASPBERRY GLAZE 1 (3-ounce/90-g) packet raspberry jell-o (jelly) crystals
• 1 cup (250 ml) boiling water • ½ cup (120 g) crushed ice • 1 cup (100 g) unsweetened shredded
(desiccated) coconut • Candy flowers and leaves, to decorate

MAKES 12 CUPCAKES • **PREPARATION** 30 MINUTES + 45 MINUTES TO CHILL & SET • **BAKING** 25–30 MINUTES

LAMINGTON CUPCAKES

CUPCAKES 1. Preheat the oven to 325°F (170°C/gas 3). Line a 12-cup muffin pan with paper liners. Sift the flour, baking powder, and salt into a bowl.

2. Beat the butter, sugar, and vanilla in a bowl until pale and creamy. Add the eggs one at a time, beating until just blended after each addition. Beat in the flour mixture, alternating with the milk. Spoon the batter into the paper liners, filling each one two-thirds full.

3. Bake for 25–30 minutes, until golden brown and a toothpick inserted into the centers comes out clean. Transfer the muffin pan to a wire rack. Let cool completely before removing the cupcakes.

RASPBERRY GLAZE 4. Mix the jell-o crystals and water in a bowl until dissolved. Add the ice and let it melt. Chill in the refrigerator for 15 minutes, stirring often, until the jell-o has set slightly.

5. Dip the tops of the cupcakes into the raspberry jell-o, turning to coat completely. Then dip them in the coconut, turning to coat. Decorate with a candy flower. Let set for at least 30 minutes before serving.

★ *THESE CUPCAKES ARE INSPIRED BY THE TRADITIONAL AUSTRALIAN FOAM CAKES CALLED LAMINGTONS.*

● **IF YOU LIKED THIS RECIPE, TRY THE ICE CREAM CUPCAKES ON PAGE 24.**

CUPCAKES 3 ounces (90 g) white chocolate, coarsely chopped • ⅓ cup (90 ml) light (single) cream • 1 cup (150 g) all-purpose (plain) flour • 1 teaspoon baking powder • ¼ teaspoon salt • ½ cup (50 g) finely ground pistachios • ⅓ cup (90 g) unsalted butter, softened • 1 cup (200 g) sugar • 2 large eggs • 2 tablespoons rose water

ROSE FROSTING ½ cup (120 g) unsalted butter, softened • 2 cups (300 g) confectioners' (icing) sugar • ½ tablespoon rose water • 12 pink candy roses, to decorate

MAKES 12 CUPCAKES • **PREPARATION** 30 MINUTES • **BAKING** 25–30 MINUTES

ROSY CUPCAKES

CUPCAKES 1. Preheat the oven to 325°F (170°C/gas 3). Line a 12-cup muffin pan with paper liners.

2. Melt the white chocolate and cream in a double boiler over barely simmering water, stirring until smooth. Set aside to cool.

3. Sift the flour, baking powder, and salt into a bowl. Stir in the pistachios. Beat the butter and sugar in a bowl until pale and creamy. Add the eggs one at a time, beating until just blended after each addition.

4. Beat in the flour mixture, chocolate mixture, and rose water. Spoon the batter into the paper liners, filling each one two-thirds full.

5. Bake for 25–30 minutes, until golden brown and a toothpick inserted into the centers comes out clean. Transfer the muffin pan to a wire rack. Let cool completely before removing the cupcakes.

ROSE FROSTING 6. Beat the butter, confectioners' sugar, and rose water in a small bowl until pale and creamy.

7. Put the frosting in a pastry (piping) bag fitted with a star nozzle. Pipe a large rosette of frosting on each cupcake and top with a candy rose.

IF YOU LIKED THIS RECIPE, TRY THE CHOCOLATE ROSE CUPCAKES ON PAGE 102.

FLORENTINE CUPCAKES

CUPCAKES 3 ounces (90 g) dark chocolate, chopped • ⅓ cup (90 ml) light (single) cream • ⅔ cup (100 g) all-purpose (plain) flour • 2 tablespoons unsweetened cocoa powder • 1 teaspoon baking powder • ½ cup (50 g) finely ground almonds • ⅓ cup (90 g) salted butter, softened • 1 cup (200 g) firmly packed dark brown sugar • 2 large eggs

CHOCOLATE GANACHE 4 ounces (120 g) dark chocolate, chopped • ¼ cup (60 ml) light (single) cream

TOPPING 2 ounces (60 g) dark chocolate, chopped • 1 cup (120 g) slivered almonds • ⅔ cup (120 g) candied (glacé) cherries, chopped • ¼ cup (45 g) candied (glacé) ginger, chopped • 2 tablespoons candied (glacé) orange peel

MAKES 12 CUPCAKES • PREPARATION 45 MINUTES + 35 MINUTES TO COOL & SET • BAKING 25-30 MINUTES

CUPCAKES **1.** Preheat the oven to 325°F (170°C/gas 3). Line a 12-cup muffin pan with paper liners.

2. Melt the chocolate and cream in a double boiler over barely simmering water. Sift the flour, cocoa, and baking powder into a bowl. Stir in the almonds.

3. Beat the butter and brown sugar in a bowl until creamy. Add the eggs one at a time, beating until just blended after each addition. Gradually beat in the flour mixture and melted chocolate. Spoon the batter into the paper liners, filling each one two-thirds full.

4. Bake for 25-30 minutes, until risen and a toothpick inserted into the centers comes out clean. Transfer the muffin pan to a wire rack. Let cool completely before removing the cupcakes.

CHOCOLATE GANACHE **5.** Melt the chocolate and cream in a double boiler over barely simmering water. Let cool for 5 minutes, then spread over the cupcakes.

TOPPING **6.** Melt the chocolate in a double boiler over barely simmering water. Set aside to cool for a few minutes.

7. Mix the slivered almonds, cherries, ginger, and orange peel in a small bowl. Cover the tops of the cupcakes with this mixture, pressing it gently into the ganache. Put the chocolate in a small plastic food bag and snip off one corner. Drizzle over the cupcakes. Let set for at least 30 minutes before serving.

• IF YOU LIKED THIS RECIPE, TRY THE CHOCOLATE HAZELNUT CUPCAKES ON PAGE 52.

TOADSTOOL CUPCAKES

CUPCAKES 1⅔ cups (250 g) all-purpose (plain) flour • 2 teaspoons baking powder • ¼ teaspoon salt • 1 cup (250 g) unsalted butter, softened • 1¼ cups (250 g) sugar • 1 teaspoon vanilla extract (essence) • 4 large eggs

FROSTING ¾ cup (180 g) salted butter, softened 2½ cups (375 g) confectioners' (icing) sugar • Red food coloring • White mini marshmallows, sliced, to decorate • Candy toadstools, to decorate (optional)

MAKES 18 CUPCAKES • **PREPARATION** 30 MINUTES + 30 MINUTES TO SET • **BAKING** 20-25 MINUTES

CUPCAKES 1. Preheat the oven to 350°F (180°C /gas 4). Line one 12-cup and one 6-cup muffin pan with white paper liners. Sift the flour, baking powder, and salt into a bowl.

2. Beat the butter, sugar, and vanilla in a bowl until pale and creamy. Add the eggs one at a time, beating until just combined after each addition. Gradually beat in the flour mixture. Spoon the batter into the paper liners, filling each one two-thirds full.

3. Bake for 20-25 minutes, until golden brown and a toothpick inserted into the centers comes out clean. Transfer the muffin pan to a wire rack. Let cool completely before removing the cupcakes.

FROSTING 4. Beat the butter and confectioners' sugar in a bowl until pale and creamy. Add enough red food coloring to make a bright red frosting. Beat until smooth and well combined.

5. Spread the red frosting evenly over the cupcakes. Top with slices of marshmallow and decorate with the candy toadstools, if using. Let set for at least 30 minutes before serving.

● **IF YOU LIKED THIS RECIPE, TRY THE BUTTERFLY CUPCAKES ON PAGE 12.**

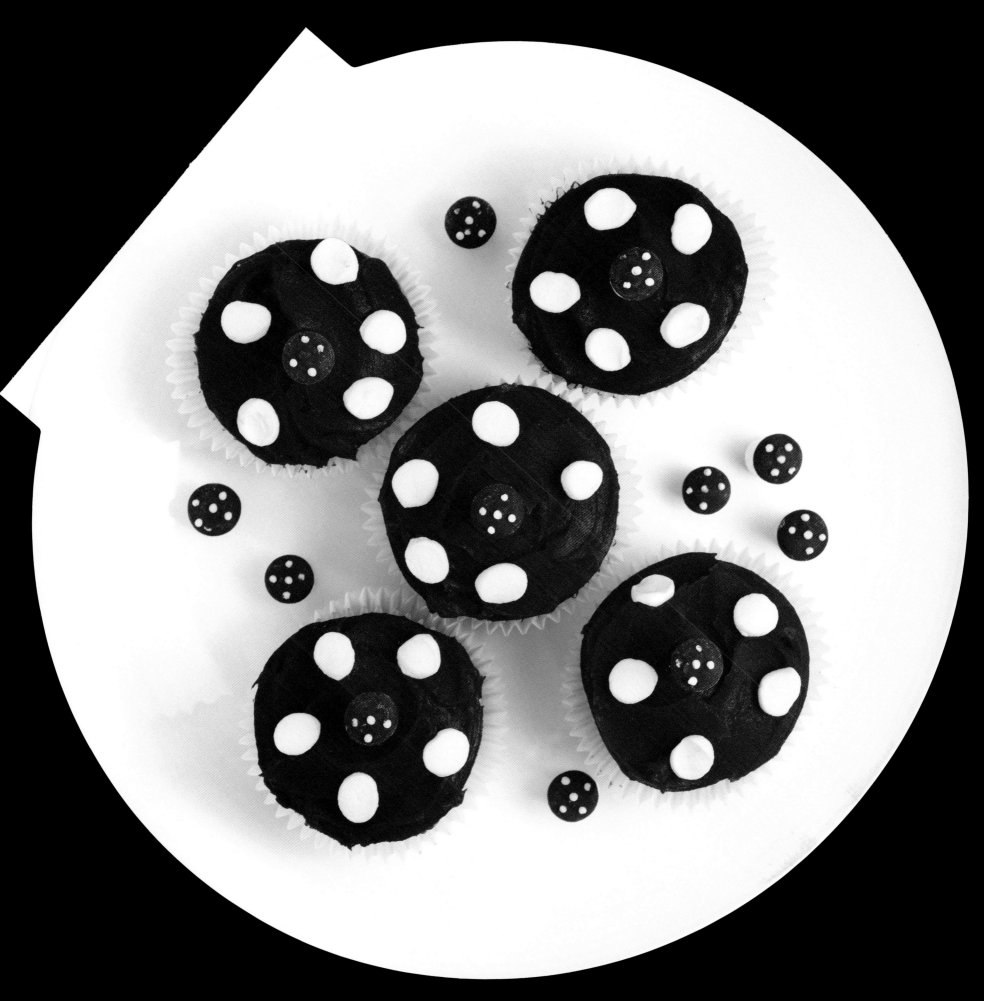

ICE CREAM CUPCAKES

CUPCAKES 1¼ cups (180 g) all-purpose (plain) flour • 1 teaspoon baking powder • 1 teaspoon ground cinnamon • ⅛ teaspoon salt • ½ cup (120 g) unsalted butter, softened • ¾ cup (150 g) sugar • ½ teaspoon vanilla extract (essence) • 2 large eggs ⅓ cup (90 ml) milk • 1 cup (150 g) raspberries • 12 flat-bottom ice cream cones

FROSTING ¾ cup (180 g) unsalted butter, softened • 2 cups (300 g) confectioners' (icing) sugar ½ teaspoon vanilla extract (essence) • Few drops red food coloring • 2 tablespoons unsweetened cocoa powder • Colored sprinkles, to decorate

MAKES 12 CUPCAKES • **PREPARATION** 30 MINUTES • **BAKING** 20–25 MINUTES

CUPCAKES 1. Preheat the oven to 350°F (180°C/gas 4). Line a 12-cup muffin pan with paper liners. Sift the flour, baking powder, cinnamon, and salt into a bowl.

2. Beat the butter, sugar, and vanilla in a bowl until pale and creamy. Add the eggs one at a time, beating until just blended after each addition. Gradually beat in the flour mixture, alternating with the milk. Stir in the raspberries. Spoon the batter into the paper liners, filling each one two-thirds full.

3. Bake for 20–25 minutes, until golden brown and a toothpick inserted into the centers comes out clean. Transfer the muffin pan to a wire rack. Let cool completely before removing the cupcakes.

4. Remove the paper liners from the cupcakes. Shape the bottoms with a serrated knife so they sit inside the ice cream cones. Place the cupcakes in the cones.

FROSTING 5. Beat the butter, confectioners' sugar, and vanilla in a bowl until smooth.

6. Divide the frosting evenly among three small bowls. Add the red food coloring to one, stir the cocoa into another, and leave the third one plain.

7. Spread the frostings over the cupcakes, creating four of each color. Finish with the colored sprinkles.

● IF YOU LIKED THIS RECIPE, TRY THE TOADSTOOL CUPCAKES ON PAGE 22.

SPIDERMAN CUPCAKES

CUPCAKES

1⅓ cups (200 g) all-purpose (plain) flour • 1½ teaspoons baking powder • ⅛ teaspoon salt • ½ cup (120 g) unsalted butter, softened • 1 cup (200 g) firmly packed light brown sugar • 1 teaspoon vanilla extract (essence) • 2 large eggs • ½ cup (120 ml) milk warmed

DECORATION

8 ounces (250 g) yellow fondant • ½ cup (150 g) apricot preserves (jam), 4 ounces (120 g) red fondant • Black gel food frosting pen • 2 ounces (60 g) white fondant Blue frosting and silver cachous (balls), to decorate plate (optional)

MAKES 12 CUPCAKES • **PREPARATION** 1 HOUR • **BAKING** 20–25 MINUTES

CUPCAKES

1. Preheat the oven to 350°F (180°C/gas 4). Line a 12-cup muffin pan with bright blue paper liners. Sift the flour, baking powder, and salt into a bowl.

2. Beat the butter, brown sugar, and vanilla in a bowl until creamy. Add the eggs one at a time, beating until just blended after each addition. Gradually beat in the flour mixture, alternating with the milk. Spoon the batter into the paper liners, filling each one two-thirds full.

3. Bake for 20–25 minutes, until golden brown and a toothpick inserted into the centers comes out clean. Transfer the muffin pan to a wire rack. Let cool completely before removing the cupcakes.

DECORATION

4. Roll the yellow fondant out to ⅛ inch (3 mm) thick. Use a cookie cutter or glass to cut out 12 circles just large enough to cover the cupcakes. Brush the tops of the cupcakes with apricot preserves and cover with the fondant, pressing down to make it stick. Roll out the red fondant to ⅛ inch (3 mm) thick and cut out 12 ovals. Moisten with a little warm water and stick on each cupcake.

5. Use the black gel food frosting pen to draw a spider's web pattern on the red fondant. Roll out the white fondant to ⅛ inch (3 mm) thick and cut out superman eye-shaped pieces. Place two on each red oval to resemble the eyes.

★ COLORED, READY-TO-USE FONDANT IS AVAILABLE AT BAKING SUPPLY STORES OR FROM ONLINE SUPPLIERS.

● **IF YOU LIKED THIS RECIPE, TRY THE SUPERMAN CUPCAKES ON PAGE 46.**

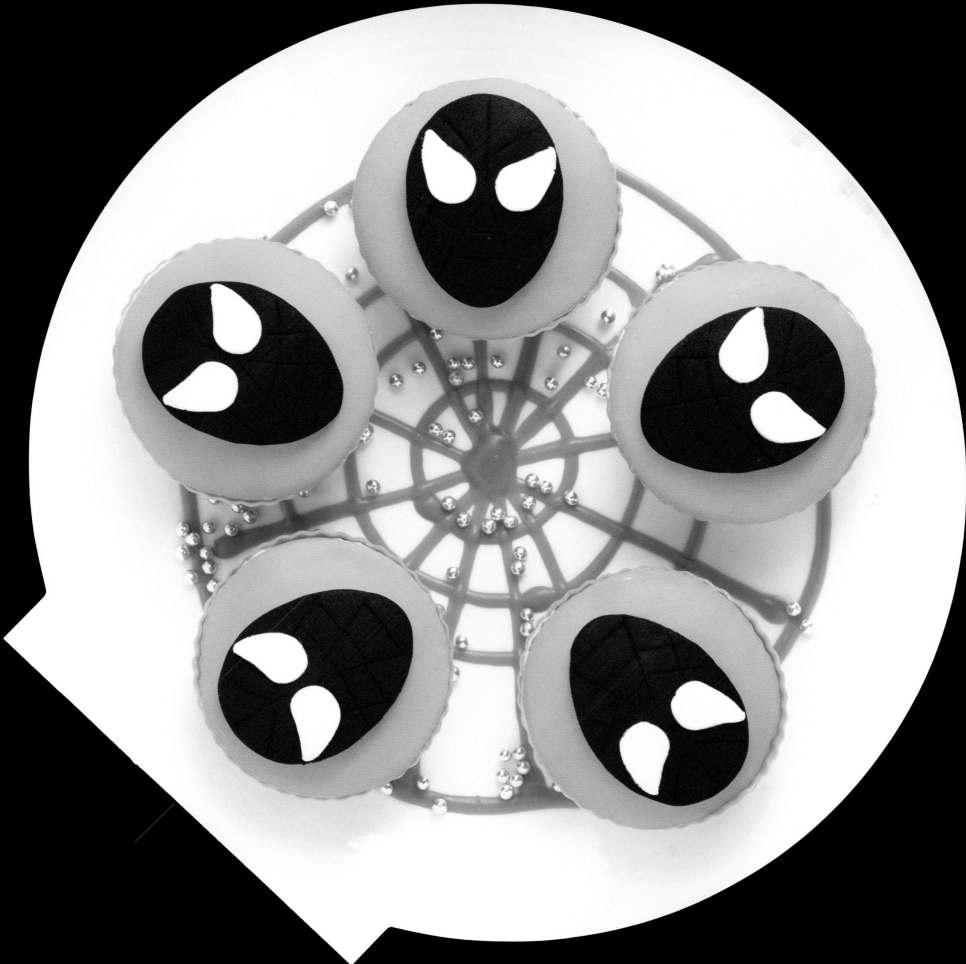

MERINGUE CUPCAKES

CUPCAKES 4 large white eggs • 1 teaspoon vanilla extract (essence) • ½ teaspoon cream of tartar • 1¼ cups (250 g) superfine (caster) sugar

TOPPING 8 ounces (250 g) cream cheese, softened • 1 cup (250 ml) Greek-style yogurt, chilled overnight in a cheesecloth-lined sieve set in a bowl • 3 tablespoons confectioners' (icing) sugar • ½ cup (75 g) red currants • 2 tablespoons kirsch • ¼ cup (50 g) superfine (caster) sugar Silver cachous (balls), to decorate

MAKES 20-24 CUPCAKES • **PREPARATION** 45 MINUTES • **BAKING** 1 HOUR

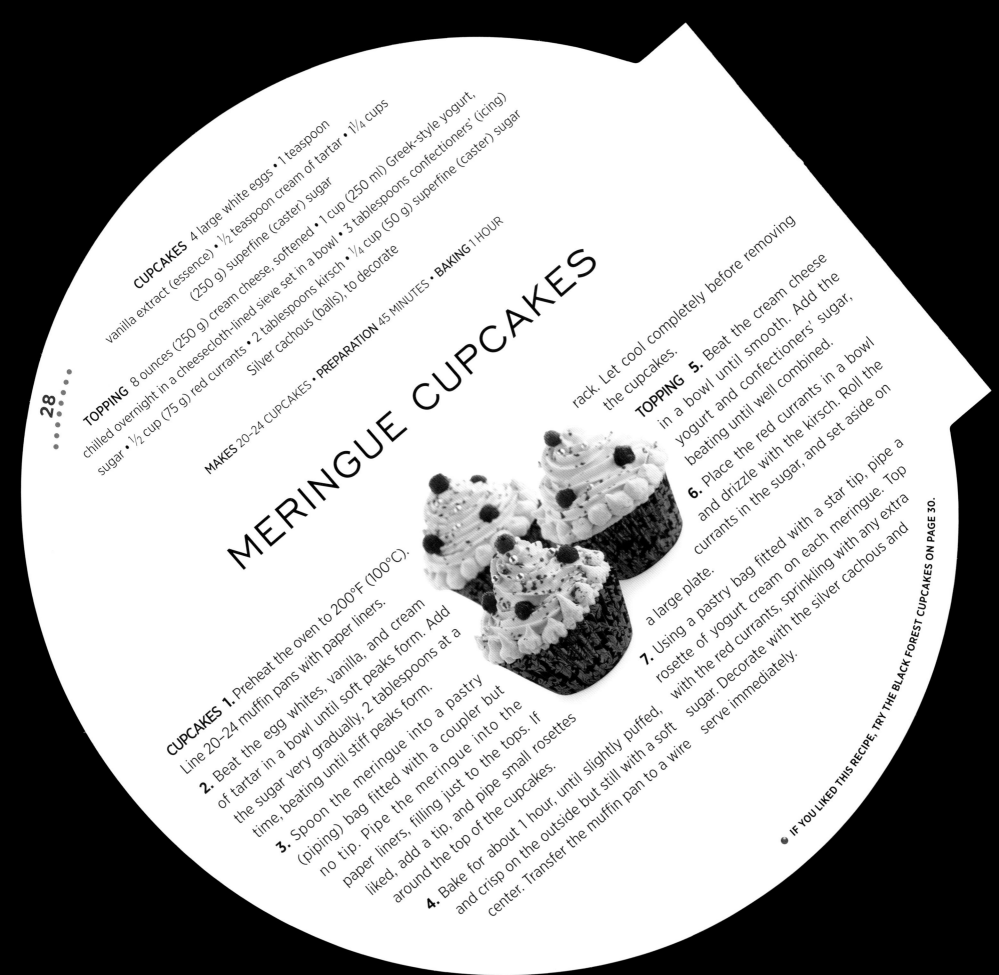

CUPCAKES 1. Preheat the oven to 200°F (100°C). Line 20-24 muffin pans with paper liners.

2. Beat the egg whites, vanilla, and cream of tartar in a bowl until soft peaks form. Add the sugar very gradually, 2 tablespoons at a time, beating until stiff peaks form.

3. Spoon the meringue into a pastry (piping) bag fitted with a coupler but no tip. Pipe the meringue into the paper liners, filling just to the tops. If liked, add a tip, and pipe small rosettes around the top of the cupcakes.

4. Bake for about 1 hour, until slightly puffed, and crisp on the outside but still with a soft center. Transfer the muffin pan to a wire

rack. Let cool completely before removing the cupcakes.

TOPPING 5. Beat the cream cheese in a bowl until smooth. Add the yogurt and confectioners' sugar, beating until well combined.

6. Place the red currants in a bowl and drizzle with the kirsch. Roll the currants in the sugar, and set aside on a large plate.

7. Using a pastry bag fitted with a star tip, pipe a rosette of yogurt cream on each meringue. Top with the red currants, sprinkling with any extra sugar. Decorate with the silver cachous and serve immediately.

IF YOU LIKED THIS RECIPE, TRY THE BLACK FOREST CUPCAKES ON PAGE 30.

BLACK FOREST CUPCAKES

CUPCAKES 3 ounces (90 g) dark chocolate, chopped • ⅓ cup (90 ml) light (single) cream 1 cup (150 g) all-purpose (plain) flour • 2 tablespoons unsweetened cocoa powder • 1 teaspoon baking powder • ⅛ teaspoon salt • ⅓ cup (90 g) unsalted butter, softened • 1 cup (200 g) sugar • 2 large eggs • 2 tablespoons kirsch ½ cup (120 g) drained maraschino cherries, chopped

TOPPING ⅔ cup (150 ml) heavy (double) cream • 2 tablespoons confectioners' (icing) sugar ½ tablespoon kirsch • Chocolate sprinkles, to finish • 12 fresh cherries, to decorate

MAKES 12 CUPCAKES • **PREPARATION** 30 MINUTES • **BAKING** 20–25 MINUTES

CUPCAKES 1. Preheat the oven to 350°F (180°C /gas 4). Line a 12-cup muffin pan with paper liners.

2. Melt the chocolate and cream in a double boiler over barely simmering water, stirring until smooth. Set aside to cool. Sift the flour, cocoa, baking powder, and salt into a bowl.

3. Beat the butter and sugar in a bowl until pale and creamy. Add the eggs one at a time, beating until just blended after each addition. Gradually beat in the flour mixture, melted chocolate, and kirsch. Spoon the batter into the paper liners, filling each one two-thirds full.

4. Bake for 20–25 minutes, until risen and a toothpick inserted into the center comes out clean. Transfer the muffin pan to a wire rack. Let cool completely before removing the cupcakes.

TOPPING 5. Beat the cream in a small bowl until it begins to thicken. Add the confectioners' sugar, beating until soft peaks form. Stir in the kirsch.

6. Top each cupcake with a dollop of cream. Finish with the chocolate sprinkles and top with a cherry. Serve at once.

● **IF YOU LIKED THIS RECIPE, TRY THE CHOCOLATE RASPBERRY CUPCAKES ON PAGE 92.**

SOCCER BALL CUPCAKES

CUPCAKES 1½ cups (225 g) all-purpose (plain) flour • 3 tablespoons unsweetened cocoa powder • 1½ teaspoons baking powder • ¼ teaspoon salt • ½ cup (120 g) unsalted butter, softened • ¾ cup (150 g) firmly packed light brown sugar 1 teaspoon vanilla extract (essence) • 2 large eggs • ½ cup (120 ml) milk

FROSTING ½ cup (120 g) unsalted butter, softened • 1½ cups (225 g) confectioners' (icing) sugar ½ teaspoon vanilla extract (essence) • Few drops green food coloring • 5 ounces (150 g) white fondant 1 black candy writer

MAKES 12 CUPCAKES • PREPARATION 45 MINUTES • **BAKING** 20–25 MINUTES

CUPCAKES **1.** Preheat the oven to 350°F (180°C /gas 4). Line a 12-cup muffin pan with paper liners. Sift the flour, cocoa, baking powder, and salt into a bowl.

2. Beat the butter, brown sugar, and vanilla in a bowl until creamy. Add the eggs one at a time, beating until just blended after each addition. Gradually add the flour mixture, alternating with the milk. Spoon the batter into the paper liners, filling each one two-thirds full.

3. Bake for 20–25 minutes, until risen and a toothpick inserted into the centers comes out clean. Let cool completely before removing the cupcakes. Transfer the muffin pan to a wire rack.

FROSTING **4.** Beat the butter, confectioners' sugar, and vanilla in a bowl until smooth. Stir in the green food coloring. Spoon into a pastry (piping) bag with a small star-shaped tip and pipe small rosettes of frosting on the cupcakes.

5. Divide the fondant into 12 equal portions and shape into round balls. Place one on top of each cupcake. Use the candy writer to decorate the soccer balls.

✸ PREPARE THESE CUPCAKES FOR A YOUNG SOCCER FAN TO CELEBRATE A SPECIAL GAME.

● IF YOU LIKED THIS RECIPE, TRY THE PIRATE CUPCAKES ON PAGE 50.

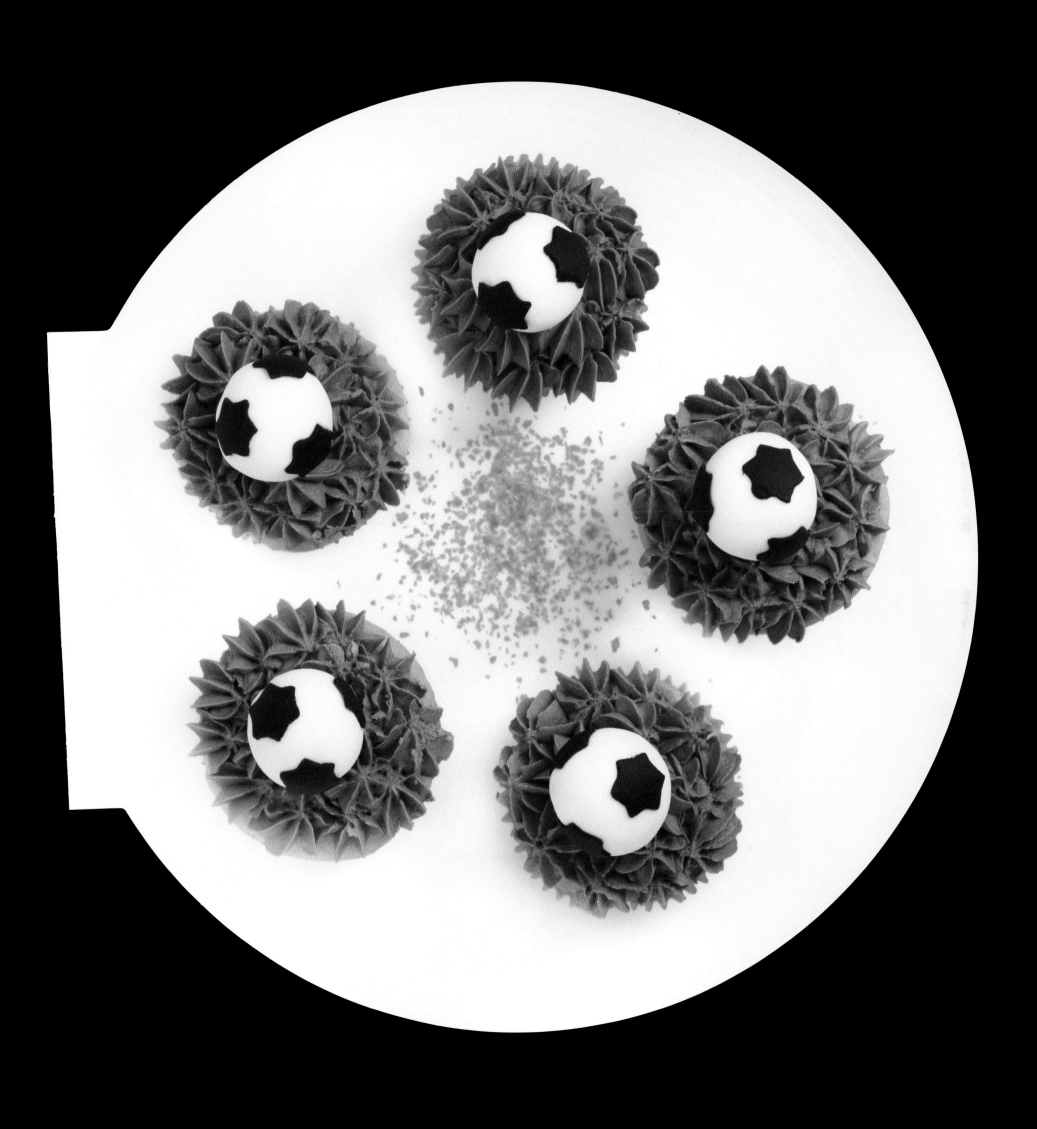

CLOWN CUPCAKES

CUPCAKES 1½ cups (225 g) all-purpose (plain) flour • 2 teaspoons baking powder • ½ teaspoon ground cinnamon • ⅛ teaspoon vanilla extract (essence) • ½ cup (120 ml) light (single) cream ½ teaspoon salt • 1 cup (200 g) sugar • 2 large eggs Few drops red food coloring

FROSTING 2 cups (300 g) confectioners' (icing) sugar • 1–2 tablespoons boiling water • Red candy writer • 24 small yellow candy-coated chocolates • 12 red candy-coated chocolates (M&M's or Smarties) 3 ounces (90 g) dark chocolate • 4 ice cream wafers, cut into 12 triangles

MAKES 12 CUPCAKES • **PREPARATION** 45 MINUTES • **BAKING** 20–25 MINUTES

CUPCAKES 1. Preheat the oven to 350°F (180°C/gas 4). Line a 12-cup muffin pan with paper liners. Sift the flour, baking powder, cinnamon, and salt into a bowl.

2. Beat the sugar, eggs, and vanilla in a bowl until pale and thick. Gradually beat in the flour mixture, alternating with the cream. Divide the mixture evenly between two bowls. Stir the red food coloring into one to make a bright red batter. Put alternate spoonfuls of batter into the paper liners, filling each one two-thirds full.

3. Bake for 20–25 minutes, until a toothpick inserted into the centers comes out clean. Transfer the muffin pan to a wire rack. Let cool completely before removing the cupcakes.

FROSTING 4. Stir the confectioners' sugar and water in a small bowl to make a smooth frosting. Spread over the cupcakes.

5. Make the clown faces: Use the candy writer draw a small red cross on each cupcake, where you will place the left eye. Use the small candy-coated eye and a larger red candy-coated cupcake. Use the candy writer to draw chocolates for eyes and a larger candy-coated chocolate for the nose. Use the candy writer to draw the mouth.

6. Melt the chocolate in a double boiler over barely simmering water, or in the microwave. Spoon the chocolate into a small plastic food bag and snip off one corner. Drizzle the wafer triangles with the chocolate. Position as the clowns' hat, securing with a little melted chocolate.

● **IF YOU LIKED THIS RECIPE, TRY THE BEETLE CUPCAKES ON PAGE 120.**

COCONUT & CHERRY CUPCAKES

CUPCAKES 1 cup (150 g) all-purpose (plain) flour • 1 teaspoon baking powder • ⅛ teaspoon salt • ⅓ cup (30 g) unsweetened shredded (desiccated) coconut • ¾ cup (150 g) sugar • 3 large eggs • 3½ ounces (100 g) unsalted butter, softened • ⅔ cup (150 g) candied (glacé) cherries, chopped

FROSTING 2 cups (300 g) confectioners' (icing) sugar • 1–2 tablespoons boiling water • Few drops blue food coloring • 12 red candied (glacé) cherries • 2–3 tablespoons unsweetened shredded (desiccated) coconut

MAKES 12 CUPCAKES • **PREPARATION** 30 MINUTES + 30 MINUTES TO SET • **BAKING** 20–25 MINUTES

CUPCAKES 1. Preheat the oven to 350°F (180°C /gas 4). Line a 12-cup muffin pan with bright red paper liners. Sift the flour, baking powder, and salt into a bowl. Stir in the coconut.

2. Beat the butter and sugar in a bowl until pale and creamy. Add the eggs one at a time, beating until just combined after each addition. Gradually beat in the flour mixture. Stir in the chopped candied cherries. Spoon the batter into the paper liners, each one two-thirds full.

3. Bake for 20–25 minutes, until golden brown and a toothpick inserted into the centers comes out clean. Transfer the muffin pan to a wire rack. Let cool completely before removing the cupcakes.

FROSTING 4. Mix the confectioners' sugar and water in a bowl to make a smooth frosting. Tint with blue food coloring. Spread over the cupcakes. Sprinkle with the coconut and press a candied cherry into the top of each cupcake. Let the frosting set for 30 minutes before serving.

• IF YOU LIKED THIS RECIPE, TRY THE LAMINGTON CUPCAKES ON PAGE 16.

ALPHABET CUPCAKES

CUPCAKES 1 cup (150 g) all-purpose (plain) flour • 1 teaspoon baking powder • ⅛ teaspoon salt • ⅓ cup (30 g) unsweetened shredded (desiccated) coconut • ⅓ cup (90 g) unsalted butter, softened • ½ cup (100 g) sugar • 1 teaspoon finely grated unwaxed lemon zest 2 large eggs • ¼ cup (60 ml) fresh passion fruit pulp, strained

DECORATION 8 ounces (250 g) green fondant • ½ cup (150 g) apricot preserves (jam), warmed 1 multipack (mixed colors) fondant • White candy stars (optional) • Birthday candles (optional)

MAKES 12 CUPCAKES • **PREPARATION** 1 HOUR • **BAKING** 20–25 MINUTES

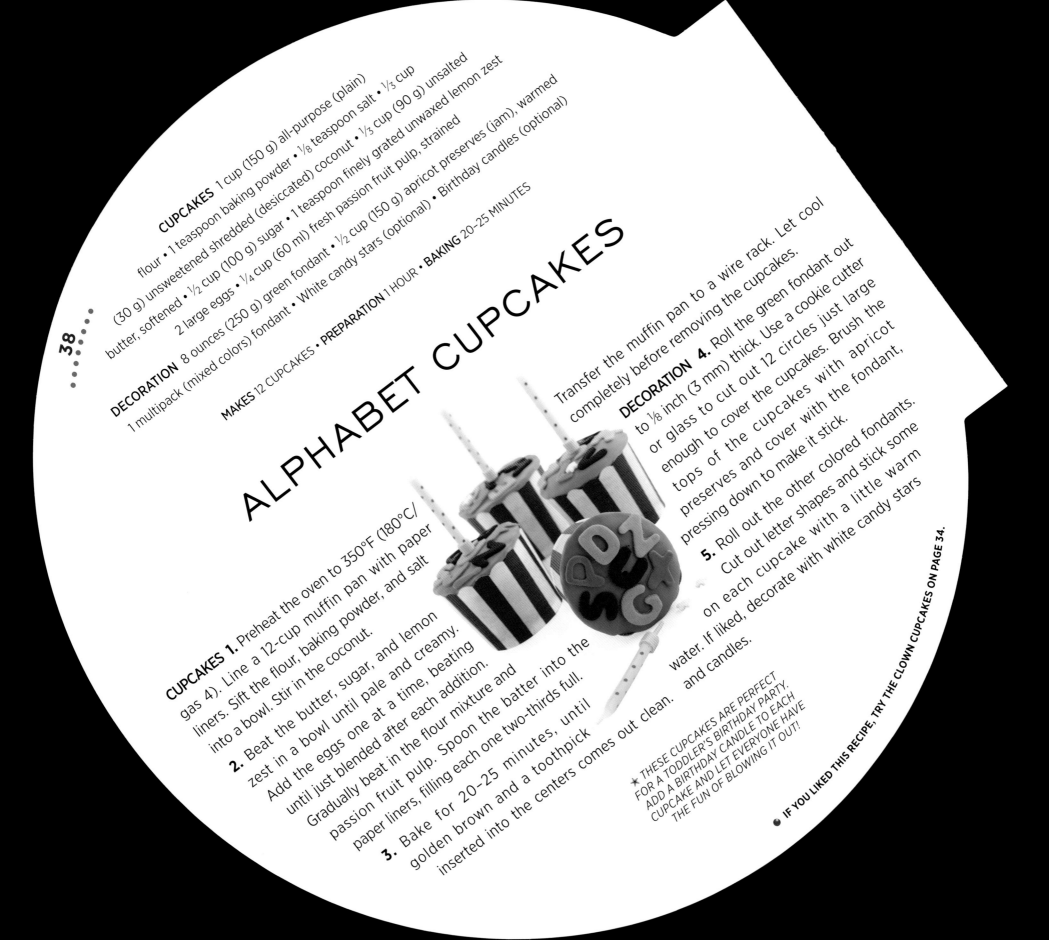

CUPCAKES 1. Preheat the oven to 350°F (180°C/gas 4). Line a 12-cup muffin pan with paper liners. Sift the flour, baking powder, and salt into a bowl. Stir in the coconut.

2. Beat the butter, sugar, and lemon zest in a bowl until pale and creamy. Add the eggs one at a time, beating until just blended after each addition. Gradually beat in the flour mixture and passion fruit pulp. Spoon the batter into the paper liners, filling each one two-thirds full.

3. Bake for 20–25 minutes, until golden brown and a toothpick inserted into the centers comes out clean.

Transfer the muffin pan to a wire rack. Let cool completely before removing the cupcakes.

DECORATION 4. Roll the green fondant out to ⅛ inch (3 mm) thick. Use a cookie cutter or glass to cut out 12 circles just large enough to cover the cupcakes. Brush the tops of the cupcakes with apricot preserves and cover with the fondant, pressing down to make it stick.

5. Roll out the other colored fondants. Cut out letter shapes and stick some on each cupcake with a little warm water. If liked, decorate with white candy stars and candles.

★ *THESE CUPCAKES ARE PERFECT FOR A TODDLER'S BIRTHDAY PARTY. ADD A BIRTHDAY CANDLE TO EACH CUPCAKE AND LET EVERYONE HAVE THE FUN OF BLOWING IT OUT!*

● IF YOU LIKED THIS RECIPE, TRY THE CLOWN CUPCAKES ON PAGE 34.

CARROT CUPCAKES

CUPCAKES 2 cups (300 g) all-purpose (plain) flour • 2 teaspoons baking soda (bicarbonate of soda) • 2 teaspoons ground cinnamon • 1 teaspoon ground ginger • ½ teaspoon ground nutmeg • ½ teaspoon salt • 2 cups (400 g) sugar • 1¼ cups (310 ml) canola oil 4 large eggs • 3 cups (300 g) finely grated carrots • ½ cup (60 g) coarsely chopped walnuts

FROSTING 1 pound (500 g) cream cheese, softened • ½ cup (120 g) salted butter, softened • 1 teaspoon vanilla extract (essence) • 2⅓ cups (350 g) confectioner's (icing) sugar • Marzipan carrots, to decorate

MAKES 24 CUPCAKES • **PREPARATION** 30 MINUTES • **BAKING** 20–25 MINUTES

CUPCAKES 1. Preheat the oven to 350°F (180°C/gas 4). Line two 12-cup muffin pans with paper liners. Sift the flour, baking soda, cinnamon, ginger, nutmeg, and salt into a bowl.

2. Beat the sugar and oil in a large bowl until combined. Add the eggs one at a time, beating until just combined after each addition. Gradually beat in the flour mixture. Stir in the carrots and walnuts. Spoon the batter into the paper liners, filling each one two-thirds full.

3. Bake for 20–25 minutes, until golden brown and a toothpick inserted into the centers comes out clean. Transfer the muffin pans to wire racks. Let cool completely before removing the cupcakes.

FROSTING 4. Beat the cream cheese, butter, and vanilla in a bowl until smooth. Gradually add the confectioner's sugar, beating until smooth and fluffy. Top with

5. Spread the frosting over the cupcakes. Top with a marzipan carrot.

✳ *PRETTY MARZIPAN CARROTS ARE AVAILABLE FROM BAKING SUPPLY STORES AND ONLINE SUPPLIERS IN MANY PARTS OF THE WORLD. IF YOU CAN'T FIND THEM, YOU COULD MAKE THEM YOURSELF USING ORANGE FONDANT, OR JUST LEAVE THEM OUT.*

● **IF YOU LIKED THIS RECIPE, TRY THE PEAR & PECAN CUPCAKES ON PAGE 88.**

EASTER CUPCAKES

CUPCAKES 1½ cups (225 g) all-purpose (plain) flour • 3 tablespoons unsweetened cocoa powder • 1½ teaspoons baking powder • ⅛ teaspoon salt • 1 cup (200 g) sugar • 2 large eggs 1 teaspoon vanilla extract (essence) • ½ cup (120 ml) heavy (double) cream ½ cup (90 g) milk chocolate chips

BUTTERCREAM 4 ounces (120 g) dark chocolate • ½ cup (120 g) salted butter, softened • ¼ teaspoon vanilla extract (essence) • ½ tablespoon milk • 1 cup (150 g) confectioners' (icing) sugar • 12 mini Easter eggs

MAKES 12 CUPCAKES • PREPARATION 30 MINUTES • BAKING 20–25 MINUTES

CUPCAKES **1.** Preheat the oven to 350°F (180°C/gas 4). Line a 12-cup muffin pan with paper liners. Sift the flour, cocoa, baking powder, and salt into a bowl.

2. Beat the sugar, eggs, and vanilla in a bowl until pale and thick. Gradually beat in the flour mixture and cream. Stir in the chocolate chips. Spoon the batter into the paper liners, filling each one two-thirds full.

3. Bake for 20–25 minutes, until a toothpick inserted into the centers comes out clean. Transfer the muffin pan to a wire rack. Let cool completely before removing the cupcakes.

BUTTERCREAM **4.** Melt the chocolate in a double boiler over barely simmering water, or in the microwave. Set aside to cool.

5. Beat the butter and vanilla in a small bowl until pale and creamy. Add the milk and chocolate, beating until just blended. Gradually add the confectioners' sugar, beating until blended.

6. Put the buttercream in a pastry (piping) bag and pipe a swirl on top of each cupcake. Top with an Easter egg.

● IF YOU LIKED THIS RECIPE, TRY THE CHOCOLATE HAZELNUT CUPCAKES ON PAGE 52.

CUPCAKES 1½ cups (225 g) all-purpose (plain) flour • 2 teaspoons baking powder • ⅛ teaspoon salt 1 cup (200 g) sugar • 2 large eggs • ½ teaspoon vanilla extract (essence) 1 teaspoon finely grated unwaxed lemon zest • ½ cup (120 ml) light (single) cream
MERINGUE FROSTING ¾ cup (150 g) + 2 tablespoons sugar • ⅓ cup (90 ml) water 1 tablespoon light corn (golden) syrup • 3 large egg whites • Jelly beans, to decorate Silver cachous (balls), to decorate the plate (optional)

MAKES 12 CUPCAKES • **PREPARATION** 45 MINUTES • **BAKING** 20–25 MINUTES

JELLY BEAN CUPCAKES

CUPCAKES 1. Preheat the oven to 350°F (180°C/gas 4). Line a standard 12-cup muffin pan with paper liners. Sift the flour, baking powder, and salt into a bowl.

2. Beat the sugar, eggs, vanilla, and lemon zest in a bowl until pale and thick. Gradually beat in the flour mixture, alternating with the cream. Spoon the batter into the paper liners, filling each one two-thirds full.

3. Bake for 20–25 minutes, until golden brown and a toothpick inserted into the centers comes out clean. Transfer the muffin pan to a wire rack. Let cool completely before removing the cupcakes.

MERINGUE FROSTING 4. Combine ¾ cup (150 g) sugar with the water and corn syrup in a small saucepan. Bring to a boil over medium heat, stirring occasionally, until the sugar dissolves. Simmer, without stirring, until the syrup reaches the soft ball stage (about 240°F/120°C). Remove from the heat.

5. Beat the egg whites until soft peaks form. Beat in the remaining 2 tablespoons of sugar. Trickle the syrup into the egg white mixture in a slow, steady stream. Beat until completely cool and stiff (but not dry) peaks form, 5–7 minutes.

6. Spoon the meringue onto the cupcakes and top with jelly beans.

IF YOU LIKED THIS RECIPE, TRY THE CHOCOLATE CANDY CUPCAKES ON PAGE 108.

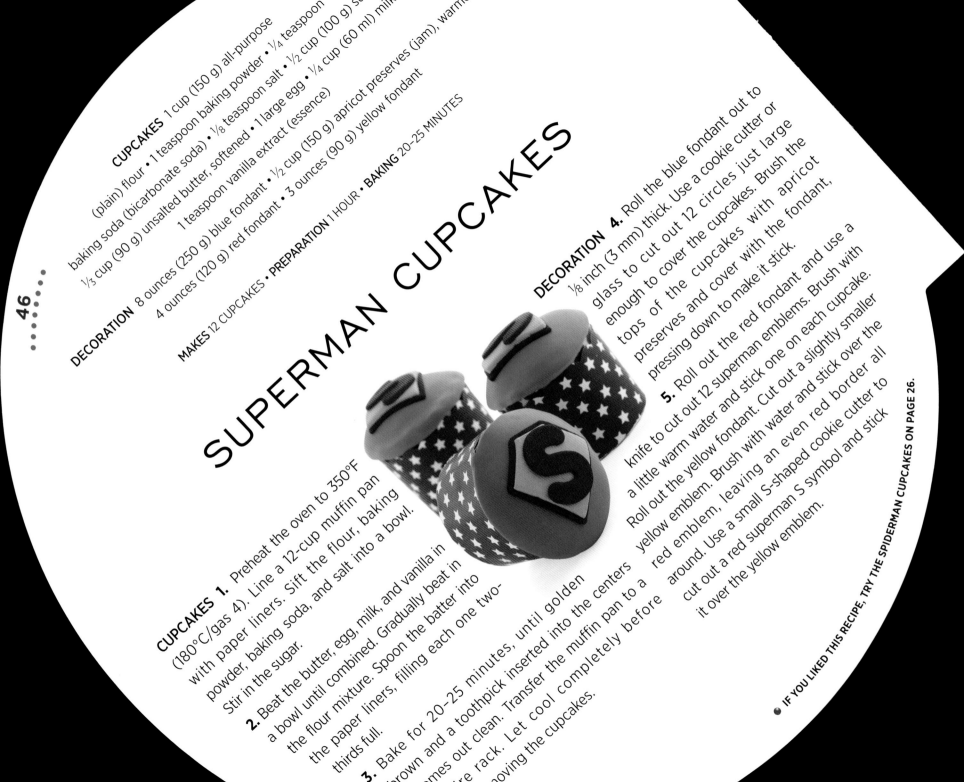

SUPERMAN CUPCAKES

CUPCAKES 1 cup (150 g) all-purpose (plain) flour • 1 teaspoon baking powder • ¼ teaspoon baking soda (bicarbonate soda) • ⅛ teaspoon salt • ½ cup (100 g) sugar • ⅓ cup (90 g) unsalted butter, softened • 1 large egg • ¼ cup (60 ml) milk • 1 teaspoon vanilla extract (essence)

DECORATION 8 ounces (250 g) blue fondant • ½ cup (150 g) apricot preserves (jam), warmed • 4 ounces (120 g) red fondant • 3 ounces (90 g) yellow fondant

MAKES 12 CUPCAKES • **PREPARATION** 1 HOUR • **BAKING** 20–25 MINUTES

CUPCAKES 1. Preheat the oven to 350°F (180°C/gas 4). Line a 12-cup muffin pan with paper liners. Sift the flour, baking powder, baking soda, and salt into a bowl. Stir in the sugar.

2. Beat the butter, egg, milk, and vanilla in a bowl until combined. Gradually beat in the flour mixture. Spoon the batter into the paper liners, filling each one two-thirds full.

3. Bake for 20–25 minutes, until golden brown and a toothpick inserted into the centers comes out clean. Transfer the muffin pan to a wire rack. Let cool completely before removing the cupcakes.

DECORATION 4. Roll the blue fondant out to ⅛ inch (3 mm) thick. Use a cookie cutter or glass to cut out 12 circles just large enough to cover the cupcakes. Brush the tops of the cupcakes with apricot preserves and cover with the fondant, pressing down to make it stick.

5. Roll out the red fondant and use a knife to cut out 12 superman emblems. Brush with a little warm water and stick one on each cupcake. Roll out the yellow fondant. Cut out a slightly smaller yellow emblem. Brush with water and stick over the red emblem, leaving an even red border all around. Use a small S-shaped cookie cutter to cut out a red superman S symbol and stick it over the yellow emblem.

IF YOU LIKED THIS RECIPE, TRY THE SPIDERMAN CUPCAKES ON PAGE 26.

ORANGE POPPY SEED CUPCAKES

CUPCAKES 1⅓ cups (200 g) self-rising flour • ⅓ cup (30 g) poppy seeds • ½ cup (30 g) finely ground almonds • ¼ cup (150 g) sugar • 1 tablespoon finely grated unwaxed orange zest • ¾ cup (120 g) unsalted butter, softened • 2 large eggs • ½ cup (120 ml) freshly squeezed orange juice

FROSTING 2 cups (300 g) confectioners' (icing) sugar • 1–2 tablespoons freshly squeezed orange juice • ¼ cup (30 g) poppy seeds

DECORATION Zest of 3 unwaxed oranges, in long thin strips • ¼ cup (50 g) sugar + extra • ¼ cup (60 ml) water

MAKES 12 CUPCAKES • **PREPARATION** 45 MINUTES • **BAKING** 20–25 MINUTES

CUPCAKES 1. Preheat the oven to 325°F (170°C/gas 3). Line a 12-cup muffin pan with paper liners. Sift the flour into a bowl. Stir in the almonds and poppy seeds.

2. Beat the butter, sugar, and orange zest in a bowl until pale and creamy. Add the eggs one at a time, beating until just blended after each addition. Gradually beat in the flour mixture, alternating with the orange juice. Spoon the batter into the paper liners, filling each one two-thirds full.

3. Bake for 20–25 minutes, until golden brown and a toothpick inserted into the centers comes out clean. Transfer the muffin pan to a wire rack. Let cool completely before removing the cupcakes.

FROSTING 4. Mix the confectioners' sugar and orange juice in a bowl until smooth. Spread over the cupcakes. Sprinkle with the poppy seeds.

DECORATION 5. Bring a small saucepan of water to a boil. Blanch the orange zest in the boiling water for 30 seconds. Drain.

6. Heat the sugar and water in a small saucepan over medium heat, stirring until the sugar dissolves. Increase the heat to high and boil for 2 minutes. Add the orange zest, decrease the heat to low, and simmer for 10 minutes. Set aside to cool in the syrup.

7. Remove the orange zest and drain on a clean cloth. Toss the zest in the extra sugar. Arrange on the cupcakes.

IF YOU LIKED THIS RECIPE, TRY THE BLUEBERRY CUPCAKES ON PAGE 10.

CUPCAKES 1⅓ cups (200 g) all-purpose (plain) flour • 1 teaspoon baking powder 1 teaspoon ground cinnamon • ¼ teaspoon baking soda (bicarbonate of soda) ⅛ teaspoon salt • ½ cup (100 g) firmly packed dark brown sugar • ⅓ cup (90 g) unsalted butter, softened • 2 large eggs • ¼ cup (60 ml) milk • 1 teaspoon vanilla extract
DECORATION ½ cup (120 g) unsalted butter, softened • ½ teaspoon vanilla extract (essence) • 1½ cups (225 g) confectioners' (icing) sugar • 5 ounces (150 g) red fondant • Black, red, and yellow candy writers White and blue candy dots, for eyes

MAKES 12 CUPCAKES • **PREPARATION** 1 HOUR • **BAKING** 20–25 MINUTES

PIRATE CUPCAKES

CUPCAKES 1. Preheat the oven to 350°F (180°C/gas 4). Line a 12-cup muffin pan with paper liners. Sift the flour, baking powder, cinnamon, baking soda, and salt into a bowl. Stir in the brown sugar.

2. Beat the butter, eggs, milk, and vanilla in a bowl until combined. Gradually beat in the flour mixture. Spoon the batter into the paper liners, filling each one two-thirds full.

3. Bake for 20–25 minutes, until golden brown. Transfer the muffin pan to a wire rack. Let cool completely before removing the cupcakes.

DECORATION 4. Beat the butter, vanilla, and confectioners' sugar in a small bowl. Spread over the cupcakes.

5. Roll the red fondant out to ⅛ inch (3 mm) thick. Use a cookie cutter or glass to cut out six rounds of red fondant the same size as the tops of the cupcakes. Cut the rounds in half. Place a half round of red fondant on each cupcake. Cut out 2 small ties for each red bandana and stick on the corners with a little warm water.

6. Use the black candy writer to add the eye patch, the red one for the mouths, and the yellow one for the spots on the bandanas. Add a white candy dot and a blue dot to make the eye next to the patch.

● IF YOU LIKED THIS RECIPE, TRY THE CLOWN CUPCAKES ON PAGE 34.

CHOCOLATE HAZELNUT CUPCAKES

CUPCAKES 3 ounces (90 g) dark chocolate, coarsely chopped • ⅓ cup (90 ml) light (single) cream • ⅔ cup (100 g) all-purpose (plain) flour • ⅛ teaspoon salt • 2 tablespoons unsweetened cocoa powder • 1 teaspoon baking powder • ⅓ cup (50 g) finely ground hazelnuts • ⅓ cup (90 g) unsalted butter, softened • 1 cup (200 g) firmly packed light brown sugar • 2 large eggs • 1 tablespoon hazelnut liqueur • ¼ cup (40 g) hazelnuts, coarsely chopped

FROSTING 4 ounces (120 g) dark chocolate, coarsely chopped • ¾ cup (120 g) chocolate hazelnut spread (such as Nutella) • 36 toasted hazelnuts, to decorate • Yellow sprinkles

MAKES 12 CUPCAKES • **PREPARATION** 30 MINUTES + 30 MINUTES TO SET • **BAKING** 25–30 MINUTES

CUPCAKES 1. Preheat the oven to 325°F (170°C/gas 3). Line a 12-cup muffin pan with paper liners.

2. Melt the chocolate and cream in a double boiler over barely simmering water. Set aside to cool. Sift the flour, cocoa, baking powder, and salt into a small bowl. Stir in the ground hazelnuts.

3. Beat the butter and brown sugar in a bowl until creamy. Add the eggs one at a time, beating until just blended after each addition. Gradually beat in the flour mixture and melted chocolate. Stir in the liqueur and chopped hazelnuts. Spoon the batter into the paper liners, filling each one two-thirds full.

4. Bake for 25–30 minutes, until risen and a toothpick inserted into the centers comes out clean. Transfer the muffin pan to a wire rack. Let cool completely before removing the cupcakes.

FROSTING 5. Melt the chocolate in a double boiler over barely simmering water, or in the microwave. Remove from the heat and stir in the chocolate hazelnut spread. Let cool a little.

6. Spoon the frosting into a pastry (piping) bag fitted with a star nozzle and pipe a swirl onto each cupcake. Decorate with the toasted hazelnuts and a few sprinkles. Let set for 30 minutes before serving.

● **IF YOU LIKED THIS RECIPE, TRY THE DEVIL'S FOOD CUPCAKES ON PAGE 80.**

CUPCAKES 1 cup (150 g) all-purpose (plain) flour • 1 teaspoon baking powder • 1 teaspoon pumpkin pie spice or allspice • ⅛ teaspoon salt • ½ cup (120 ml) sunflower oil • ½ cup (100 g) firmly packed light brown sugar • 2 large eggs • 1 teaspoon finely grated unwaxed orange zest • ½ cup (120 g) grated butternut squash or pumpkin

DECORATION 1½ cups (225 g) confectioners' (icing) sugar • 1–2 tablespoons water • Few drops orange food coloring • 1 tube black frosting • Halloween candy and decorations, to serve

MAKES 12 CUPCAKES • **PREPARATION** 30 MINUTES + 30 MINUTES TO SET • **BAKING** 25–30 MINUTES

JACK-O'-LANTERN CUPCAKES

CUPCAKES 1. Preheat the oven to 325°F (170°C/gas 3). Line a 12-cup muffin pan with paper liners. Sift the flour, baking powder, pumpkin pie spice, and salt into a small bowl.

2. Combine the oil, brown sugar, eggs, and orange zest in a bowl. Stir in the pumpkin, followed by the flour mixture. Spoon the batter into the paper liners, filling each one two-thirds full.

3. Bake for 25–30 minutes, until golden brown and a toothpick inserted into the centers comes out clean. Transfer the muffin pan to a wire rack. Let cool completely before removing the cupcakes.

DECORATION 4. Combine the confectioners' sugar with enough of the water in a small bowl to make a smooth frosting. Add the orange food coloring.

5. Spread the frosting over the cupcakes. Fit the tube of black frosting with a tip and pipe Jack-o'-Lantern faces on each cupcake. Let set for 30 minutes before serving.

● IF YOU LIKED THIS RECIPE, TRY THE TABBY CAT CUPCAKES ON PAGE 126.

CUPCAKES 3 ounces (90 g) dark chocolate, coarsely chopped • ⅓ cup (90 ml) light (single) cream • 1 cup (150 g) all-purpose (plain) flour • 2 tablespoons unsweetened cocoa powder 1 teaspoon baking powder • ⅛ teaspoon salt • 1 cup (200 g) firmly packed brown sugar ⅓ cup (90 g) unsalted butter, softened • 1 teaspoon vanilla extract (essence) • 2 large eggs **FROSTING** 2 cups (300 g) confectioners' (icing) sugar • ½ cup (120 g) salted butter, melted 2 teaspoons coffee extract (essence) • 1–2 tablespoons water • 3 Mars bars, sliced, to decorate

MAKES 12 CUPCAKES • **PREPARATION** 30 MINUTES + 30 MINUTES TO SET • **BAKING** 25–30 MINUTES

MARS BAR CUPCAKES

CUPCAKES 1. Preheat the oven to 325°F (170°C/gas 3). Line a 12-cup muffin pan with paper liners.

2. Melt the chocolate and cream in a double boiler over barely simmering water. Set aside to cool a little. Sift the flour, cocoa, baking powder, and salt into a small bowl.

3. Beat the brown sugar, butter, and vanilla in a bowl until creamy. Add the eggs one at a time, beating until just blended after each addition. Gradually beat in the flour mixture and chocolate mixture. Spoon the batter into the paper liners, filling each one two-thirds full.

4. Bake for 25–30 minutes, until risen and a toothpick inserted into the centers comes out clean. Transfer the muffin pan to a wire rack. Let cool completely before removing the cupcakes.

FROSTING 5. Beat the confectioners' sugar, butter, coffee extract, and enough of the water in a small bowl to make a creamy frosting.

6. Spread the frosting over the cupcakes. Top each one with slices of Mars bar, piling them up. Let the set for 30 minutes before serving.

● IF YOU LIKED THIS RECIPE, TRY THE CARAMEL CUPCAKES ON PAGE 68.

LAVENDER CUPCAKES

CUPCAKES 1⅓ cups (200 g) all-purpose (plain) flour • 1 teaspoon baking powder • 2 tablespoons dried lavender flowers • ⅔ cup (150 g) sugar • 2 large eggs (150 g) salted butter • ¾ cup confectioners' (icing) sugar • ½ teaspoon lavender extract • Few drops purple food coloring • Purple sugar, to sprinkle 12 sprigs fresh or dried lavender, to decorate

FROSTING 2 cups (300 g) confectioners' (icing) sugar • 2 large eggs 1-2 tablespoons boiling water

MAKES 12 CUPCAKES • **PREPARATION** 30 MINUTES + 30 MINUTES TO SET • **BAKING** 20-25 MINUTES

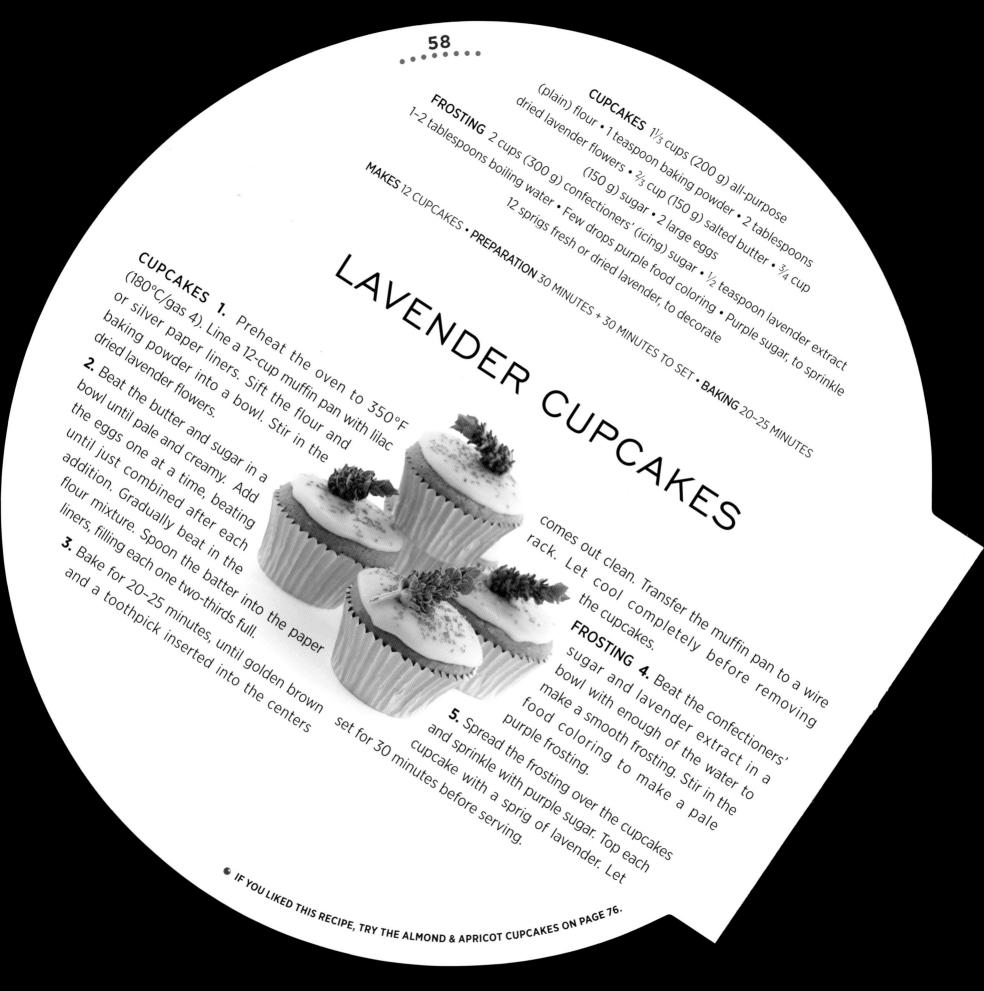

CUPCAKES 1. Preheat the oven to 350°F (180°C/gas 4). Line a 12-cup muffin pan with lilac or silver paper liners. Sift the flour and baking powder into a bowl. Stir in the dried lavender flowers.

2. Beat the butter and sugar in a bowl until pale and creamy. Add the eggs one at a time, beating until just combined after each addition. Gradually beat in the flour mixture. Spoon the batter into the paper liners, filling each one two-thirds full.

3. Bake for 20-25 minutes, until golden brown and a toothpick inserted into the centers comes out clean. Transfer the muffin pan to a wire rack. Let cool completely before removing the cupcakes.

FROSTING 4. Beat the confectioners' sugar and lavender extract in a bowl with enough of the water to make a smooth frosting. Stir in the food coloring to make a pale purple frosting.

5. Spread the frosting over the cupcakes and sprinkle with purple sugar. Top each cupcake with a sprig of lavender. Let set for 30 minutes before serving.

● IF YOU LIKED THIS RECIPE, TRY THE ALMOND & APRICOT CUPCAKES ON PAGE 76.

CHRISTMAS CUPCAKES

CUPCAKES ½ cup (90 g) candied (glacé) cherries, chopped • ½ cup (90 g) dried figs, finely chopped • ½ cup (90 g) raisins • 3 tablespoons brandy • 1 cup (150 g) all-purpose (plain) flour • 1½ teaspoons baking powder • 1 teaspoon ground cinnamon • ⅛ teaspoon salt • ½ cup (120 g) unsalted butter, softened • ¾ cup (150 g) firmly packed light brown sugar • 2 teaspoons finely grated unwaxed orange zest • 2 large eggs

DECORATION 8 ounces (250 g) white fondant • ⅓ cup (100 g) orange marmalade, warmed and strained • Readymade holly and berry decorations

MAKES 12 CUPCAKES • **PREPARATION** 45 MINUTES + 15 MINUTES TO SOAK • **BAKING** 20-25 MINUTES

CUPCAKES 1. Preheat the oven to 375°F (190°C/gas 5). Line a 12-cup muffin pan with paper liners.

2. Put the cherries, figs, and raisins in a small bowl with the brandy. Let sit for 15 minutes. Sift the flour, baking powder, cinnamon, and salt into a small bowl.

3. Beat the butter, brown sugar, and orange zest in a bowl until creamy. Add the eggs one at a time, beating until just blended. Gradually beat in the flour mixture and dried fruit and brandy. Spoon the batter into the paper liners, filling each one two-thirds full.

4. Bake for 20-25 minutes, until golden brown and a toothpick inserted into the centers comes out clean. Transfer the muffin pan to a wire rack. Let cool completely before removing the cupcakes.

DECORATION 5. Roll out the white fondant to ⅛ inch (3 mm) thick. Using a cookie cutter or glass, cut out rounds large enough to cover the tops of the cupcakes.

6. Brush the cupcakes with the marmalade and place the fondant rounds on top, pressing down gently to make them stick. Finish each cupcake with some holly and berry decorations.

✻ THERE ARE SO MANY PRETTY CHRISTMAS DECORATIONS AVAILABLE NOW. YOU COULD DECORATE THESE CUPCAKES WITH FATHER CHRISTMAS FIGURES, REINDEER, SNOWMEN, CHRISTMAS TREES OR STARS, OR ANYTHING ELSE THAT YOU LIKE.

● IF YOU LIKED THIS RECIPE, TRY THE NEW YEAR CUPCAKES ON PAGE 70.

PISTACHIO CUPCAKES

CUPCAKES 1⅓ cup (200 g) self-rising flour • ½ cup (50 g) finely ground pistachios • ½ cup (120 g) salted butter, softened • ¾ cup (150 g) sugar • 2 large eggs • 2 tablespoons rose water • ½ cup (120 ml) milk

FROSTING ½ cup (120 g) salted butter, softened • 2 cups (300 g) confectioners' (icing) sugar • 1 teaspoon rose water • Few drops pink food coloring • Pistachios, to decorate

MAKES 12 CUPCAKES • PREPARATION 30 MINUTES + 30 MINUTES TO SET • BAKING 25–30 MINUTES

CUPCAKES 1. Preheat the oven to 325°F (170°C/gas 3). Line a 12-cup muffin pan with paper liners. Sift the flour into a bowl. Stir in the ground pistachios.

2. Beat the butter and sugar in a bowl until pale and creamy. Add the eggs one at a time, beating until just blended after each addition. Gradually beat in the rose water, flour mixture, and milk. Spoon the batter into the paper liners, filling each one two-thirds full.

3. Bake for 25–30 minutes, until golden brown and a toothpick inserted into the centers comes out clean. Transfer the muffin pan to a wire rack. Let cool completely before removing the cupcakes.

FROSTING 4. Beat the butter, confectioners' sugar, and rose water in a small bowl until well blended. Tint with a few drops of pink food coloring.

5. Fit a pastry (piping) bag with a ¼-inch (5-mm) star tip. Fill with the frosting and pipe over the cupcakes. Sprinkle with the pistachios. Let set for 30 minutes before serving.

● IF YOU LIKED THIS RECIPE, TRY THE ORANGE POPPY SEED CUPCAKES ON PAGE 48.

MINT CHOCOLATE CUPCAKES

CUPCAKES 1¼ cups (180 g) all-purpose (plain) flour • ½ cup (75 g) unsweetened cocoa powder • ¾ teaspoon baking soda (bicarbonate of soda) • ¼ teaspoon salt • 1 cup (200 g) sugar • ⅓ cup (90 ml) vegetable oil • 1 large egg • 1 teaspoon vanilla extract (essence) • ¾ cup (180 ml) milk • ½ cup (90 g) mint chocolate chips

MINT BUTTERCREAM ⅔ cup (150 g) salted butter • 2 cups (300 g) confectioners' (icing) sugar 2-3 tablespoons milk • ½ teaspoon peppermint extract (essence) • Few drops green food coloring Mint-flavored candies, to decorate

MAKES 12 CUPCAKES • **PREPARATION** 30 MINUTES • **BAKING** 20-25 MINUTES

CUPCAKES 1. Preheat the oven to 350°F (180°C/gas 4). Line a 12-cup muffin pan with paper liners. Sift the flour, cocoa, baking soda, and salt into a bowl.

2. Beat the sugar, oil, egg, and vanilla in a bowl until smooth. Gradually beat in the flour mixture, alternating with the milk. Stir in the mint chocolate chips. Spoon the batter into the paper liners, filling each one two-thirds full.

3. Bake for 20-25 minutes, until springy to the touch and a toothpick inserted into the centers comes out clean. Transfer the muffin pan to a wire rack. Let cool completely before removing the cupcakes.

MINT BUTTERCREAM 4. Beat the butter in a bowl until very pale and creamy. Beat in the confectioners' sugar, milk, and peppermint extract until smooth and creamy. Stir in enough food coloring to make a bright green frosting.

5. Spoon the frosting into a pastry (piping) bag and pipe over the cupcakes. Decorate with the mint-flavored candies.

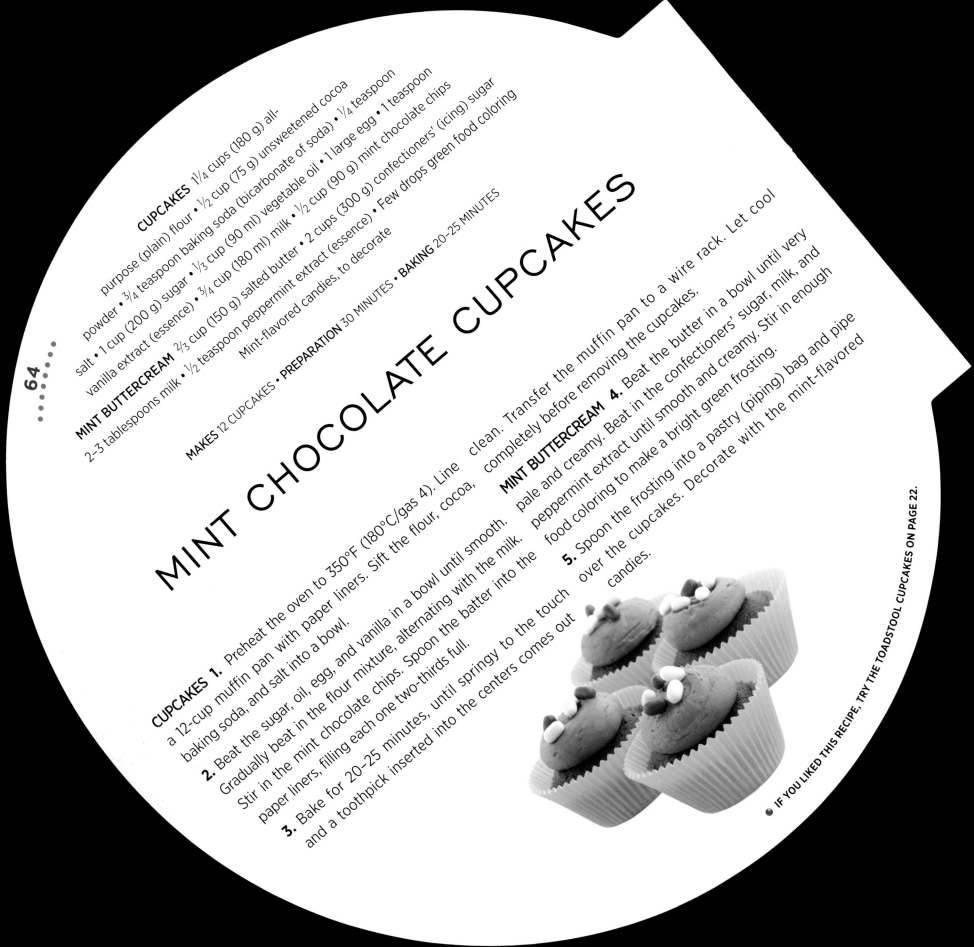

IF YOU LIKED THIS RECIPE, TRY THE TOADSTOOL CUPCAKES ON PAGE 22.

COMING-OF-AGE CUPCAKES

CUPCAKES 2 cups (200 g) finely ground pecans • 1¼ cups (250 g) sugar • ¼ cup (30 g) unsweetened cocoa powder • 1 teaspoon baking powder • 1 teaspoon ground cinnamon • ⅛ teaspoon salt • 4 large eggs • ½ cup (120 ml) melted unsalted butter • 1 teaspoon vanilla extract (essence) • 1 teaspoon finely grated unwaxed orange zest **CHOCOLATE GANACHE** 7 ounces (200 g) dark chocolate, chopped • ⅓ cup (90 ml) heavy (double) cream **DECORATION** 1 cup (150 g) confectioners' (icing) sugar • 1 tablespoon water • 12 candy hearts with birthday number • 12 candles

MAKES 12 CUPCAKES • **PREPARATION** 45 MINUTES • **BAKING** 25–30 MINUTES

CUPCAKES 1. Preheat the oven to 325°F (170°C/gas 3). Line a 12-cup muffin pan with paper liners.

2. Combine the pecans, sugar, cocoa, baking powder, cinnamon, and salt in a bowl. Beat the eggs, butter, vanilla, and orange zest in another bowl. Pour the egg mixture into the pecan mixture and stir until just combined. Spoon the batter into the paper liners, filling each one two-thirds full.

3. Bake for 25–30 minutes, until golden brown and a toothpick inserted into the centers comes out clean. Transfer the muffin pan to a wire rack. Let cool completely before removing the cupcakes.

CHOCOLATE GANACHE 4. Melt the chocolate and cream in a double boiler over barely simmering water, stirring until smooth. Remove from the heat. Set aside to cool and thicken. Spread over the cupcakes.

DECORATION 5. Mix the confectioners' sugar and water in a small bowl, stirring until smooth. Spoon into a small plastic food bag and snip off a tiny corner. Pipe a row of decorative dots around the edges of the cupcakes. Top with the candy hearts and a candle.

★ THESE CUPCAKES CAN BE SERVED ON ANY BIRTHDAY. JUST CHANGE THE BIRTHDAY NUMBER TO SUIT.

● IF YOU LIKED THIS RECIPE, TRY THE GRADUATION DAY CUPCAKES ON PAGE 90.

CUPCAKES 1⅔ cups (250 g) all-purpose (plain) flour • 1½ teaspoons baking powder • ¼ teaspoon salt • ½ cup (120 g) unsalted butter, softened • 1 cup (200 g) firmly packed light brown sugar • 1 teaspoon vanilla extract (essence) • 2 large eggs • ⅔ cup (150 ml) milk
FROSTING ½ cup (120 g) salted butter, softened • ¼ cup (60 ml) dulce de leche 2 cups (300 g) confectioners' (icing) sugar • White sprinkles

MAKES 12 CUPCAKES • **PREPARATION** 30 MINUTES + 30 MINUTES TO SET • **BAKING** 20–25 MINUTES

CARAMEL CUPCAKES

CUPCAKES 1. Preheat the oven to 350°F (180°C/gas 4). Line a 12-cup muffin pan with paper liners. Sift the flour, baking powder, and salt into a bowl.

2. Beat the butter and brown sugar in a bowl until creamy. Beat in the vanilla then add the eggs one at a time, beating until just combined after each addition. Gradually beat in the flour mixture, alternating with the milk. Spoon the batter into the paper liners, filling each one two-thirds full.

3. Bake for 20–25 minutes, until a toothpick inserted into the centers comes out clean. Transfer the muffin pan to a wire rack. Let cool completely before removing the cupcakes.

FROSTING 4. Beat the butter in a bowl until pale. Add the dulce de leche, then gradually beat in the confectioners' sugar.

5. Spoon the frosting into a pastry (piping) bag and pipe over the cupcakes. Top with the sprinkles. Let set for 30 minutes before serving.

● IF YOU LIKED THIS RECIPE, TRY THE SALTED PEANUT CUPCAKES ON PAGE 122.

NEW YEAR CUPCAKES

MAKES 12 CUPCAKES • **PREPARATION** 30 MINUTES • **BAKING** 20–25 MINUTES

CUPCAKES 1⅓ cups (200 g) all-purpose (plain) flour • 1½ teaspoons baking powder • ½ teaspoon ground cinnamon • ⅛ teaspoon salt • ⅓ cup (30 g) finely ground almonds 1 cup (200 g) sugar • 2 large eggs • 1 teaspoon finely grated unwaxed orange zest 1 teaspoon vanilla extract (essence) • ½ cup (120 ml) light (single) cream • ⅓ cup

CHOCOLATE ORANGE GANACHE 7 ounces (200 g) dark chocolate, coarsely chopped (90 ml) heavy (double) cream • 2 teaspoons finely grated unwaxed orange zest • Small silver cachous (balls), to decorate • 12 sparklers, to decorate • 12 milk chocolate squares

CUPCAKES 1. Preheat the oven to 350°F (180°C/gas 4). Line a 12-cup muffin pan with silver paper liners. Sift the flour, baking powder, cinnamon, and salt into a bowl. Stir in the almonds.

2. Beat the sugar, eggs, orange zest, and vanilla in a bowl until pale and thick. Gradually beat in the flour mixture, alternating with the cream. Spoon half the batter into the paper liners. Place a square of chocolate in the center and spoon in the remaining batter, filling each one two-thirds full.

3. Bake for 20–25 minutes, until golden brown and a toothpick inserted into the centers comes out clean. Transfer the muffin pan to a wire rack. Let cool completely before removing the cupcakes.

CHOCOLATE ORANGE GANACHE
4. Melt the chocolate and cream in a double boiler over barely simmering water, stirring until smooth. Remove from the heat, stir in the orange zest, and let cool.

5. Spread the ganache over the cupcakes. Cut the sparklers down to a shorter size and insert into the cupcakes. Sprinkle with silver cachous. Light when ready to serve.

IF YOU LIKED THIS RECIPE, TRY THE CHRISTMAS CUPCAKES ON PAGE 60.

CHEESECAKE CUPCAKES

BASE 12 large plain chocolate cookies, crushed • ¼ cup (60 g) unsalted butter, melted

FILLING 1 pound (500 g) cream cheese • 1½ tablespoons cornstarch (cornflour) • ½ cup (100 g) sugar • 1 teaspoon vanilla extract (essence) • 1 large egg + 1 large egg yolk • ¼ cup (60 ml) sour cream • 1 cup (150 g) fresh raspberries

DECORATION ½ cup (120 ml) heavy (double) cream • 2 teaspoons sugar • 3 ounces (90 g) dark chocolate, chopped

MAKES 10-12 CUPCAKES • PREPARATION 30 MINUTES + 4-12 HOURS TO COOL & CHILL • BAKING 20 MINUTES

BASE 1. Preheat the oven to 350°F (180°C/gas 4). Line a 12-cup muffin pan with paper liners. **2.** Mix the cookie crumbs in a bowl with the melted butter until well combined. Press the mixture into the bases of the paper liners.

FILLING 3. Beat the cream cheese in a bowl until smooth, then add the cornstarch, sugar, vanilla, egg and egg yolk, and sour cream, beating until well combined. **4.** Reserve 12 raspberries to garnish. Divide the rest evenly among the paper liners. Spoon the cream cheese mixture over the top, pressing it down gently with the back of the spoon. **5.** Bake for 20 minutes, until the filling is set, but still slightly wobbly in the center. Remove the cupcakes from the oven and set aside to cool for 30 minutes. **6.** Chill for at least 4 hours, or overnight.

DECORATION 7. Beat the cream and sugar until thickened. Place a dollop on each cupcake. Melt the chocolate in a double boiler over barely simmering water, or in the microwave. Place in a small plastic food bag, snip off one corner, and drizzle over the cupcakes. Top with a raspberry.

● IF YOU LIKED THIS RECIPE, TRY THE LEMON MERINGUE CUPCAKES ON PAGE 104.

BIRTHDAY CUPCAKES

CUPCAKES 1 cup (150 g) all-purpose (plain) flour • 3 tablespoons unsweetened cocoa powder • 1 teaspoon baking powder • ⅛ teaspoon salt • ½ cup (120 g) unsalted butter, softened • ¾ cup (150 g) firmly packed dark brown sugar • ½ teaspoon vanilla extract (essence) • 2 large eggs • 3 tablespoons milk • 3½ ounces (100 g) mini marshmallows, chopped

CHOCOLATE BUTTERCREAM 3 ounces (90 g) dark chocolate • ½ cup (120 g) unsalted butter, softened • ¼ teaspoon vanilla extract (essence) • ½ tablespoon milk • 1 cup (150 g) confectioners' (icing) sugar

DECORATION Candy-coated chocolates (M&M's or Smarties) • Colored sprinkles • 12 birthday candles

MAKES 12 CUPCAKES • **PREPARATION** 40 MINUTES • **BAKING** 20-25 MINUTES

CUPCAKES 1. Preheat the oven to 350°F (180°C/gas 4). Line a 12-cup muffin pan with colorful paper liners. Sift the flour, cocoa, baking powder, and salt into a bowl.

2. Beat the butter, brown sugar, and vanilla in a bowl until creamy. Add the eggs one at a time, beating until just blended after each addition. Gradually beat in the flour mixture, alternating with the milk. Stir in the marshmallows. Spoon the batter into the paper liners, filling each one two-thirds full.

3. Bake for 20-25 minutes, until golden brown and a toothpick inserted into the centers comes out clean. Transfer the muffin pan to a wire rack. Let cool completely before removing the cupcakes.

CHOCOLATE BUTTERCREAM 4. Melt the chocolate in a double boiler over barely simmering water, or in the microwave. Set aside to cool.

5. Beat the butter and vanilla in a bowl until pale and creamy. Pour in the milk and chocolate, beating until blended. Gradually beat in the confectioners' sugar. Spread the buttercream over the cupcakes.

DECORATION 6. Arrange the candy-coated chocolates around the edges of each cupcake. Scatter with the sprinkles. Place a candle in the center of each cupcake and light when ready to serve.

● **IF YOU LIKED THIS RECIPE, TRY THE COMING-OF-AGE CUPCAKES ON PAGE 66.**

ALMOND & APRICOT CUPCAKES

CUPCAKES 1 cup (150 g) self-rising flour • ⅓ cup (50 g) all-purpose (plain) flour • ⅛ teaspoon salt • ⅓ cup (30 g) finely ground almonds • ½ cup (120 g) unsalted butter, softened • ¾ cup (150 g) firmly packed light brown sugar • ½ teaspoon vanilla extract (essence) • 2 large eggs • ½ cup (120 ml) milk • ½ cup (90 g) dried apricots, finely chopped + extra, to decorate • ¼ cup (40 g) flaked almonds + extra, to decorate

BUTTERCREAM ½ cup (120 g) unsalted butter, softened • ¼ teaspoon vanilla extract (essence) • ½ tablespoon milk • 1 cup (150 g) confectioners' (icing) sugar

MAKES 12 CUPCAKES • **PREPARATION** 20 MINUTES • **BAKING** 20–25 MINUTES

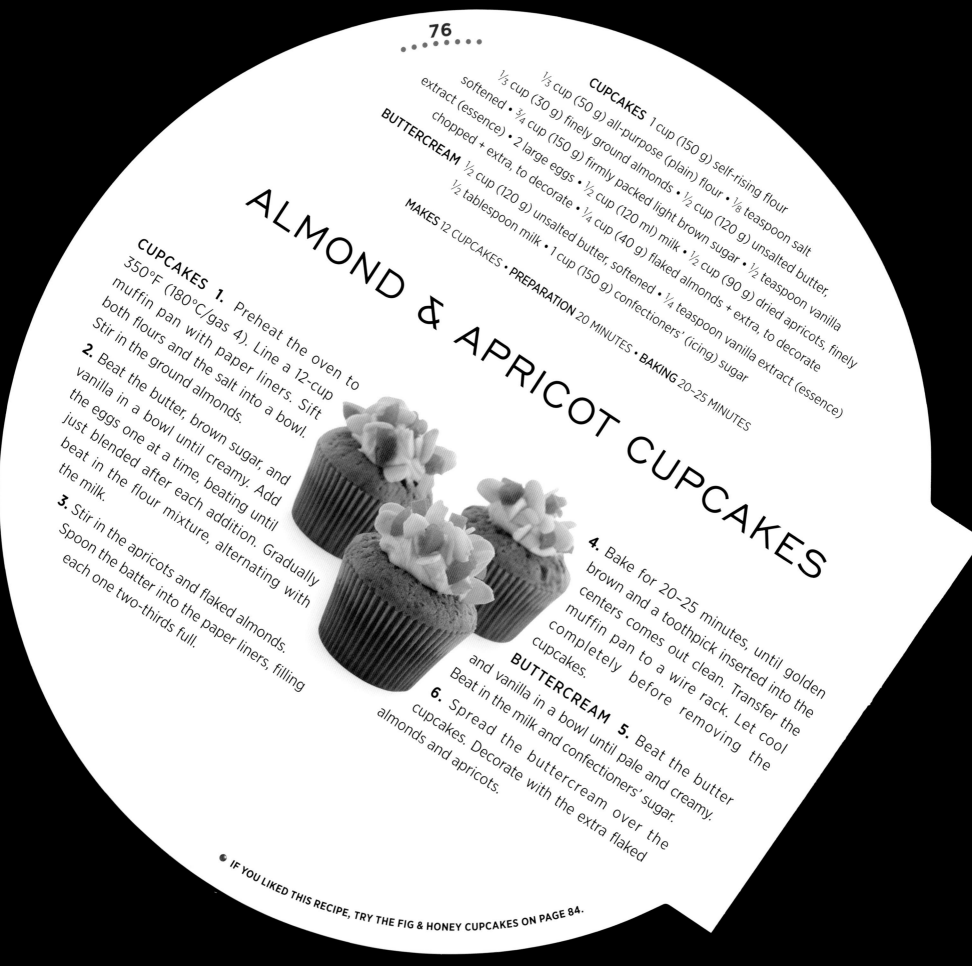

CUPCAKES 1. Preheat the oven to 350°F (180°C/gas 4). Line a 12-cup muffin pan with paper liners. Sift both flours and the salt into a bowl. Stir in the ground almonds.

2. Beat the butter, brown sugar, and vanilla in a bowl until creamy. Add the eggs one at a time, beating until just blended after each addition. Gradually beat in the flour mixture, alternating with the milk.

3. Stir in the apricots and flaked almonds. Spoon the batter into the paper liners, filling each one two-thirds full.

4. Bake for 20–25 minutes, until golden brown and a toothpick inserted into the centers comes out clean. Transfer the muffin pan to a wire rack. Let cool completely before removing the cupcakes.

BUTTERCREAM 5. Beat the butter and vanilla in a bowl until pale and creamy. Beat in the milk and confectioners' sugar.

6. Spread the buttercream over the cupcakes. Decorate with the extra flaked almonds and apricots.

● **IF YOU LIKED THIS RECIPE, TRY THE FIG & HONEY CUPCAKES ON PAGE 84.**

WEDDING CUPCAKES

CUPCAKES 2 cups (300 g) all-purpose (plain) flour • 4 teaspoons baking powder • 4 teaspoons ground ginger • 4 cups (400 g) finely ground almonds • 4 teaspoons firmly packed light brown sugar • 8 large eggs • 2 tablespoons finely grated unwaxed orange zest • 3 cups (750 ml) fresh orange juice, strained • 4 tablespoons candied (glacé) ginger, finely chopped • 1 cup (200 g) sugar

DECORATION 1 cup (150 g) confectioners' (icing) sugar • 2 pounds (1 kg) white fondant • 1 cup (325 g) orange marmalade, warmed and strained • 1½ teaspoons silver lustre • 1½ teaspoons vodka

MAKES 48 CUPCAKES • **PREPARATION** 1 HOUR • **BAKING** 20–25 MINUTES

CUPCAKES 1. Preheat the oven to 350°F (180°C/gas 4). Line four 12-cup muffin pans with paper liners. Sift the flour, baking powder, and ginger into a bowl. Stir in the almonds.

2. Beat the brown sugar, eggs, and orange zest in a bowl until creamy. Gradually beat in the flour mixture and ½ cup (120 ml) of orange juice. Stir in the candied ginger. Spoon the batter into the prepared cups, filling each one two-thirds full.

3. Bake for 20–25 minutes, until golden brown and a toothpick inserted into the centers comes out clean.

4. Simmer the remaining orange juice and sugar in a small saucepan over medium-low heat until the sugar has dissolved and

the liquid is syrupy, about 5 minutes. Pierce the warm cupcakes all over with a toothpick and brush with the orange syrup. Transfer the muffin pans to a wire rack. Let cool completely before removing the cupcakes.

DECORATION 5. Dust a clean work surface with confectioners' sugar. Roll out the fondant to ⅛ inch (3 mm) thick. Roll with a spiral swirl pattern roller. Using a cookie cutter or glass, cut out rounds large enough to cover the cupcakes. Brush the cupcakes with marmalade and place the fondant rounds on top. Combine the silver lustre and vodka in a small bowl. Using a small paint brush, paint the swirl pattern with lustre and leave to dry.

● **IF YOU LIKED THIS RECIPE, TRY THE SILVER ANNIVERSARY CUPCAKES ON PAGE 94.**

DEVIL'S FOOD CUPCAKES

CUPCAKES 1½ cups (225 g) all-purpose (plain) flour • 1½ teaspoons baking powder • ¼ teaspoon salt ...ounces (120 g) dark chocolate, chopped • ¾ cup (180 g) unsalted butter, ...oftened • ¾ cup (150 g) firmly packed dark brown sugar • 2 tablespoons corn ...(golden) syrup • 2 large eggs 1–2 red chilies (chillies), seeded and very finely chopped **...COLATE FROSTING** 7 ounces (200 g) dark chocolate, chopped • 2 tablespoons dark brown sugar ⅔ cup (150 ml) sour cream • Ready-to-use red fondant or marzipan, molded into chili shapes

MAKES 12 CUPCAKES • **PREPARATION** 30 MINUTES • **BAKING** 20–25 MINUTES

CUPCAKES 1. Preheat the oven to 350°F (180°C/gas 4). Line a 12-cup muffin pan with paper liners. Sift the flour, baking powder, and salt into a bowl. Melt the chocolate in a double boiler over barely simmering water, or in the microwave. Set aside to cool.

2. Beat the butter, brown sugar, and corn syrup until creamy. Add the eggs one at a time, beating until just combined after each addition. Gradually beat in the flour mixture, chocolate, and chilies. Spoon the batter into the paper liners, filling each one two-thirds full.

3. Bake for 20–25 minutes, until firm to the touch and a toothpick inserted into the centers comes out clean. Transfer the muffin pan to a wire rack. Let cool completely before removing the cupcakes.

FROSTING 4. Melt the chocolate in a double boiler over barely simmering water, or in the microwave. Beat in the sugar until dissolved, followed by the sour cream.

5. Spread the frosting over the cupcakes and decorate with the fondant or marzipan devil's horns.

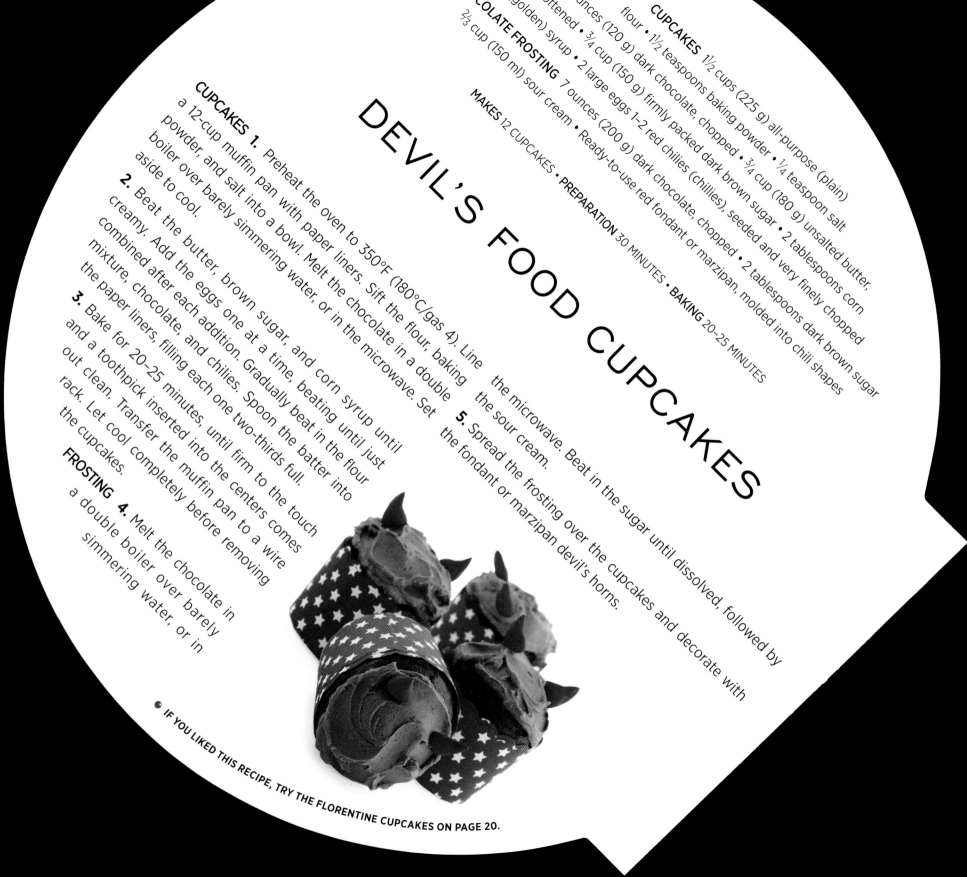

● **IF YOU LIKED THIS RECIPE, TRY THE FLORENTINE CUPCAKES ON PAGE 20.**

VALENTINE'S DAY CUPCAKES

CUPCAKES 1¼ cups (180 g) all-purpose (plain) flour • 3 tablespoons unsweetened cocoa powder • 1½ teaspoons baking powder • 1 teaspoon ground cinnamon • ⅛ teaspoon salt • ½ cup (120 g) unsalted butter, softened • ¾ cup (150 g) sugar • ½ teaspoon vanilla extract (essence) • 2 large eggs • ⅓ cup (90 ml) milk • ½ cup (90 g) dark chocolate chips • ⅓ cup (90 g) orange marmalade, warmed and strained

DECORATION 8 ounces (250 g) purple fondant • 4 ounces (120 g) red fondant • Edible gold leaf (optional)

MAKES 12 CUPCAKES • **PREPARATION** 45 MINUTES • **BAKING** 20–25 MINUTES

CUPCAKES 1. Preheat the oven to 350°F (180°C/gas 4). Line a 12-cup muffin pan with paper liners. Sift the flour, cocoa, baking powder, cinnamon, and salt into a bowl.

2. Beat the butter, sugar, and vanilla in a bowl until pale and creamy. Add the eggs one at a time, beating until just blended after each addition. Gradually beat in the flour mixture, alternating with the milk. Stir in the chocolate chips. Spoon the batter into the paper liners, filling each one two-thirds full.

3. Bake for 20–25 minutes, until risen and a toothpick inserted into the centers comes out clean. Transfer the muffin pan to a wire rack. Let cool completely before removing the cupcakes.

DECORATION 4. Roll out the purple fondant to ⅛ inch (3 mm) thick. Using a cookie cutter or glass, cut out rounds big enough to cover the tops of the cupcakes.

5. Brush the cupcakes with the marmalade and place the fondant rounds on top, pressing down gently to make them stick.

6. Mold the red fondant into heart shapes. If liked, decorate the red hearts with edible gold leaf. Place one heart on each cupcake, sticking it to the purple fondant with a little warm water.

● **IF YOU LIKED THIS RECIPE, TRY THE BRIDAL SHOWER CUPCAKES ON PAGE 86.**

FIG & HONEY CUPCAKES

CUPCAKES 1 cup (150 g) all-purpose (plain) flour • 1 teaspoon baking powder • ⅛ teaspoon salt • ½ cup (120 g) unsalted butter, softened • 1 teaspoon vanilla extract (essence) • ½ cup (100 g) sugar • ¼ cup (60 ml) honey 2 large eggs • ½ cup (90 g) finely chopped dried figs • ¼ cup (30 g) finely grated unwaxed orange zest • 3 tablespoons clear honey • ½ teaspoon vanilla finely chopped walnuts

HONEY FROSTING ⅓ cup (90 g) unsalted butter, softened • 6 dried figs, quartered extract (essence) • 1⅓ cups (200 g) confectioners' (icing) sugar

MAKES 12 CUPCAKES • **PREPARATION** 30 MINUTES • **BAKING** 20–25 MINUTES

CUPCAKES 1. Preheat the oven to 350°F (180°C/gas 4). Line a 12-cup muffin pan with paper liners. Sift the flour, baking powder, and salt into a bowl.

2. Beat the butter, sugar, honey, eggs, vanilla, and orange zest in a bowl until just blended. Beat in the flour mixture, followed by the figs and walnuts. Spoon the batter into the paper liners, filling each one two-thirds full.

3. Bake for 20–25 minutes, until golden brown and a toothpick inserted into

the centers comes out clean. Transfer the muffin pan to a wire rack. Let cool completely before removing the cupcakes.

HONEY FROSTING 4. Beat the butter, 1 tablespoon of honey, and vanilla in a small bowl. Beat in the confectioners' sugar until well blended. Spread the frosting on top of the cupcakes.

5. Decorate each cupcake with two fig quarters and drizzle with the remaining honey.

✳ IF MAKING THESE CUPCAKES DURING THE LATE SUMMER WHEN FRESH FIGS ARE IN SEASON, REPLACE THE DRIED FIGS IN THE TOPPING WITH SLICES OF SUCCULENT FRESH FIGS.

● **IF YOU LIKED THIS RECIPE, TRY THE PEAR & PECAN CUPCAKES ON PAGE 88.**

BRIDAL SHOWER CUPCAKES

CUPCAKES 4 cups (600 g) cake flour • 4 teaspoons baking powder • ½ teaspoon salt • 1⅓ cups (130 g) finely ground pistachios • 2 cups (500 g) unsalted butter, softened • 4 cups (800 g) sugar • 2 teaspoons vanilla extract (essence) • 8 large eggs • 1⅓ cups (330 ml) milk • ⅓ cup (90 ml) rose water

DECORATION • 2 pounds (1 kg) pale pink fondant • 2 pounds (1 kg) pale green fondant • 1 cup (325 g) orange marmalade, warmed and strained • Pastel colored candy flowers, to decorate

MAKES 48 CUPCAKES • **PREPARATION** 1 HOUR • **BAKING** 20–25 MINUTES

CUPCAKES **1.** Preheat the oven to 350°F (180°C/gas 4). Line four 12-cup muffin pans with silver paper liners. Sift the flour, baking powder, and salt in a large bowl. Stir in the pistachios. **2.** Beat the butter, sugar, and vanilla in a bowl until pale and creamy. Add the eggs one at a time, beating until just blended after each addition. Gradually beat in the flour mixture, milk, and rose water. Spoon the batter into the paper liners, filling each one two-thirds full. **3.** Bake for 20–25 minutes, until golden brown and a toothpick inserted into the centers comes out clean. Transfer the muffin pans to wire racks. Let cool completely before removing the cupcakes.

DECORATION **4.** Roll out the pink fondant to ⅛ inch (3 mm) thick. Use a cookie cutter or glass to cut out 48 rounds large enough to cover the cupcakes. Use a smaller cutter (about 1 inch/2.5 cm in diameter) to cut out the centers of half the pink rounds. Repeat with the green fondant. **5.** Brush the tops of the cooled cupcakes with the warm marmalade. Place the 24 full rounds of pink fondant on half the cupcakes and cover with the centers cut out. Repeat with the remaining fondant rounds of green fondant on half the cupcakes, reversing the colors. Brush with marmalade and cover with the 24 full rounds of pink fondant. **6.** Top with the candy flowers, sticking them to the fondant with a little warm water.

• **IF YOU LIKED THIS RECIPE, TRY THE WEDDING CUPCAKES ON PAGE 78.**

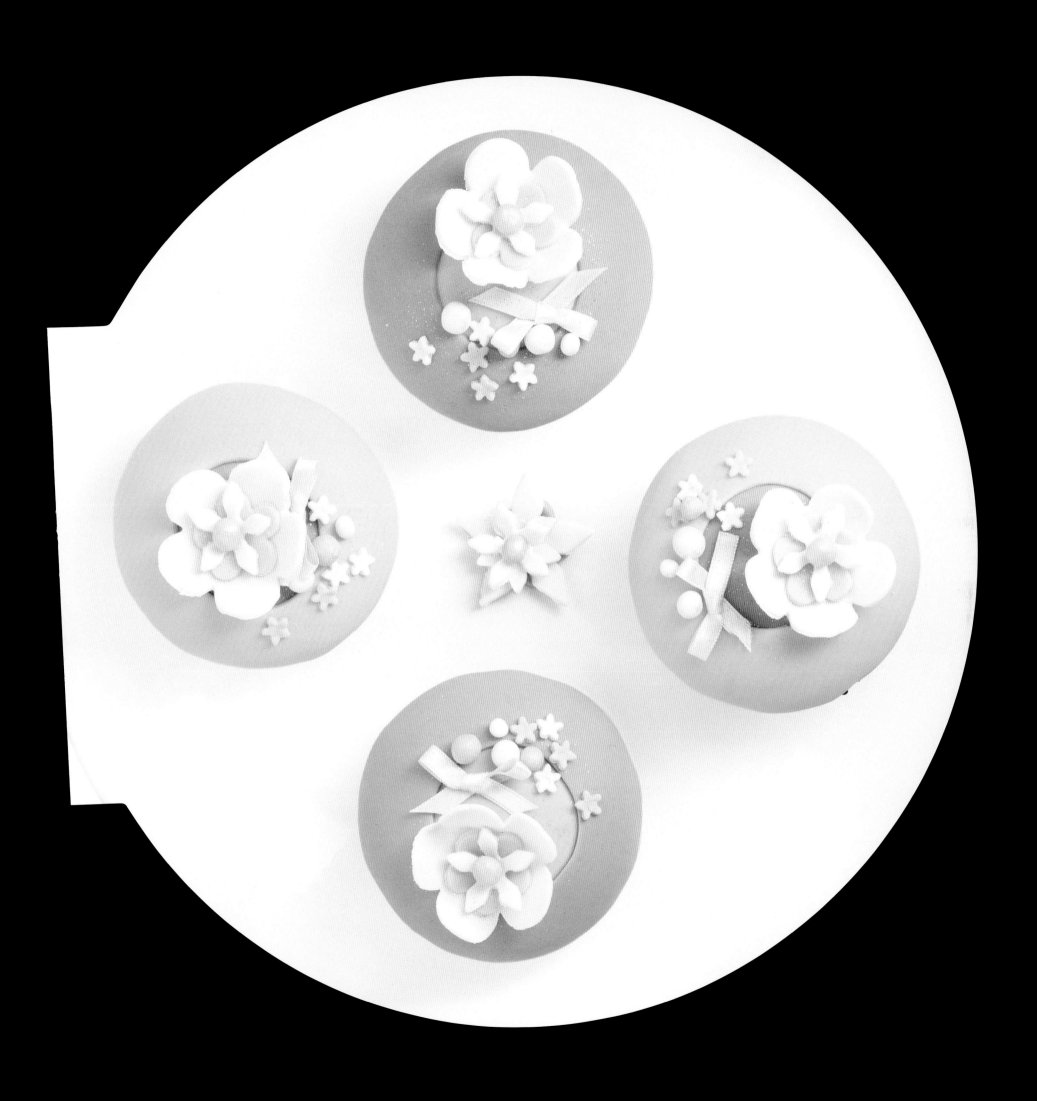

PEAR & PECAN CUPCAKES

CUPCAKES 1¾ cups (275 g) self-rising flour • ¾ cup (150 g) sugar • ⅓ cup (30 g) finely ground almonds • ¼ teaspoon salt • 1 teaspoon ground cinnamon • ¼ cup (60 g) unsalted butter, melted • ⅔ cup (150 ml) milk • 1 large egg • ¼ cup (60 g) butter, softened • ⅓ cup (35 g) coarsely chopped pecans and finely chopped • 2 small ripe pears, peeled, cored,

MAPLE FROSTING ¼ cup (60 g) butter, softened • 2 tablespoons pure maple syrup • 2 cups (300 g) confectioners' (icing) sugar • 1 tablespoon unsweetened cocoa powder • 12 pecan halves, to decorate

MAKES 12 CUPCAKES • PREPARATION 30 MINUTES + 30 MINUTES TO SET • **BAKING** 20–25 MINUTES

CUPCAKES 1. Preheat the oven to 350°F (180°C/gas 4). Line a 12-cup muffin pan with paper liners. Sift the flour, cinnamon, and salt into a bowl. Stir in the sugar and almonds.

2. Beat the milk, egg, and butter in a bowl until just blended. Stir the milk mixture into the flour mixture, followed by the pears and pecans. Spoon the batter into the paper liners, filling each one two-thirds full.

3. Bake for 20–25 minutes, until golden brown and a toothpick inserted into the centers comes out clean. Transfer the muffin pan to a wire rack. Let cool completely before removing the cupcakes.

MAPLE FROSTING 4. Beat the butter and maple syrup in a bowl until creamy. Mix in the confectioners' sugar until well blended. Divide the frosting evenly between two small bowls.

5. Fit a pastry (piping) bag with a ¼-inch (5-mm) tip. Fill with the plain frosting and pipe over half the cupcakes. Clean the pastry bag and fill with the chocolate frosting. Top each cupcake with a pecan half. Let set for 30 minutes before

6. Stir the cocoa into the other bowl of frosting. Clean the pastry bag and fill with the chocolate frosting. Top each cupcake with a pecan half. Let set for 30 minutes before

● **IF YOU LIKED THIS RECIPE, TRY THE SALTED PEANUT CUPCAKES ON PAGE 122.**

CUPCAKES 3 ounces (90 g) white chocolate, coarsely chopped • ⅓ cup (90 ml) light (single) cream • 1 cup (150 g) all-purpose (plain) flour • 1 teaspoon baking powder • ⅛ teaspoon salt • ½ cup (50 g) finely ground pistachios • ⅓ cup (90 g) unsalted butter, softened • 1 cup (200 g) sugar • ½ teaspoon vanilla extract (essence) • 2 large eggs

FROSTING ½ cup (120 g) unsalted butter, softened • ½ teaspoon vanilla extract (essence) • 1⅓ cups (200 g) confectioners' (icing) sugar • 2½ tablespoons unsweetened cocoa powder • ½ tablespoon water

DECORATION 3½ ounces (100 g) white fondant • 1 ounce (30 g) purple fondant

MAKES 12 CUPCAKES • **PREPARATION** 45 MINUTES • **BAKING** 25–30 MINUTES

GRADUATION DAY CUPCAKES

CUPCAKES 1. Preheat the oven to 325°F (170°C/gas 3). Line a 12-cup muffin pan with paper liners.

2. Melt the chocolate and cream in a double boiler over barely simmering water, stirring until smooth. Set aside to cool. Sift the flour, baking powder, and salt in a bowl. Stir in the pistachios.

3. Beat the butter, sugar, and vanilla in a bowl until pale and creamy. Add the eggs one at a time, beating until just blended after each addition. Gradually beat in the flour mixture and melted chocolate. Spoon the batter into the paper liners, filling each one two-thirds full.

4. Bake for 25–30 minutes, until risen and a toothpick inserted into the centers comes out clean. Transfer the muffin pan

to a wire rack. Let cool completely before removing the cupcakes.

FROSTING 5. Beat the butter and vanilla in a bowl until creamy. Gradually add the confectioners' sugar, cocoa, and water, beating until combined. Spread over the cupcakes.

DECORATION 6. Roll out the white fondant to ⅛ inch (3 mm) thick. Cut out twelve ¾ x 1½-inch (2 x 4-cm) rectangles. Roll up to resemble scrolls.

7. Divide the purple fondant into three pieces and roll each one into long thin "ribbons." Cut in three even lengths. Tie a ribbon around each scroll. Place on top of the cupcakes, pressing them into the frosting gently.

● IF YOU LIKED THIS RECIPE, TRY THE BULL'S EYE CUPCAKES ON PAGE 98.

CHOCOLATE RASPBERRY CUPCAKES

CUPCAKES 3 ounces (90 g) dark chocolate, coarsely chopped • ⅓ cup (90 ml) light (single) cream • ⅔ cup (100 g) all-purpose (plain) flour • 2 tablespoons unsweetened cocoa powder • 1 teaspoon baking powder • ⅛ teaspoon salt • ½ cup (50 g) finely ground almonds • ⅓ cup (90 g) unsalted butter, softened • 1 cup (200 g) sugar 2 large eggs • 1 cup (150 g) fresh raspberries **SUGARED RASPBERRIES** 1 cup (150 g) fresh raspberries 1 large egg white, lightly beaten • 2 tablespoons superfine (caster) sugar **CHOCOLATE BUTTERCREAM** 3½ ounces (100 g) dark chocolate • ½ cup (120 g) unsalted butter, softened ½ teaspoon vanilla extract (essence) ½ tablespoon milk • 1 cup (150 g) confectioners' (icing) sugar

MAKES 12 CUPCAKES • **PREPARATION** 45 MINUTES • **BAKING** 25-30 MINUTES

CUPCAKES 1. Preheat the oven to 325°F (170°C/gas 3). Line a 12-cup muffin pan with paper liners.

2. Melt the chocolate and cream in a double boiler over barely simmering water, stirring until smooth. Set aside to cool. Sift the flour, cocoa, baking powder, and salt into a bowl. Stir in the almonds.

3. Beat the butter and sugar in a bowl until pale and creamy. Add the eggs one at a time, beating until just blended after each addition. Gradually beat in the flour mixture and melted chocolate. Stir in the raspberries. Spoon the batter into the paper liners, filling each one two-thirds full.

4. Bake for 25-30 minutes, until a toothpick inserted into the centers comes out clean.

Transfer the muffin pan to a wire rack. Let cool completely before removing the cupcakes.

SUGARED RASPBERRIES 5. Line a baking sheet with parchment paper. Brush each raspberry with egg white and roll in the sugar. Place on the prepared baking sheet and leave to dry.

CHOCOLATE BUTTERCREAM 6. Melt the chocolate in a double boiler over barely simmering water, or in the microwave. Set aside to cool.

7. Beat the butter and vanilla in a bowl until pale and creamy. Add the milk and chocolate, beating until blended. Gradually beat in the confectioners' sugar.

8. Spread the buttercream over the cupcakes and top with sugared raspberries.

• IF YOU LIKED THIS RECIPE, TRY THE CHOCOLATE PEAR CUPCAKES ON PAGE 118.

SILVER ANNIVERSARY CUPCAKES

CUPCAKES 2½ cups (375 g) all-purpose (plain) flour • 1 teaspoon baking powder • ¼ teaspoon salt • 3 cups (500 g) firmly packed light brown sugar • 1 cup (250 g) unsalted butter, cubed 1¾ cups (350 g) mixed dried fruit • 3 large eggs, lightly beaten 1 teaspoon vanilla extract (essence) • ½ teaspoon almond extract (essence)

DECORATION 1 cup (150 g) confectioners' (icing) sugar • 4 pounds (2 kg) white fondant • 1 cup (325 g) orange marmalade, warmed and strained • Small white fondant or sugar flowers and bows

MAKES 32–36 CUPCAKES • PREPARATION 1½ HOURS • **BAKING** 20–25 MINUTES

CUPCAKES 1. Preheat the oven to 350°F (180°C/gas 4). Line three 12-cup muffin pans with paper liners. Sift the flour, baking powder, and salt into bowl.

2. Put the fruit in a saucepan and cover with water. Bring to a boil and simmer for 5 minutes. Drain and return the fruit to the pan.

3. Stir in the butter until melted. Add the brown sugar, eggs, and vanilla and almond extracts, stirring until combined. Spoon the batter into the paper liners, filling each one two-thirds full.

4. Bake for 20–25 minutes, until golden brown and a toothpick inserted

into the centers comes out clean. Transfer the muffin pans to wire racks. Let cool completely before removing the cupcakes.

DECORATION 5. Dust a clean work surface with confectioners' sugar. Roll out the fondant to ⅛ inch (3 mm) thick. Use a small sharp knife to cut out rounds large enough to cover the cupcakes and brush all over with marmalade. Place the fondant rounds on top. Smooth over the sides and trim the bases to fit. Decorate with the flowers, sticking them on with a little warm water.

6. Remove the paper liners from the cupcakes

● **IF YOU LIKED THIS RECIPE, TRY THE WEDDING CUPCAKES ON PAGE 78.**

STRAWBERRY CREAM CUPCAKES

CUPCAKES 1¼ cups (180 g) all-purpose (plain) flour • 1 teaspoon baking powder • ½ teaspoon ground cinnamon • ⅛ teaspoon salt • ½ cup (120 g) unsalted butter, softened • ½ cup (100 g) sugar • 1 teaspoon vanilla extract (essence) • 2 large eggs • ⅓ cup (90 ml) single (light) cream • 1 cup (150 g) fresh strawberries, finely chopped

FROSTING 2 large egg whites • ¾ cup (150 g) sugar • ¾ cup (180 g) salted butter, softened • 12 whole strawberries

MAKES 12 CUPCAKES • **PREPARATION** 30 MINUTES + 15 MINUTES TO SET • **BAKING** 20–25 MINUTES

CUPCAKES 1. Preheat the oven to 350°F (180°C/gas 4). Line a 12-cup muffin pan with paper liners. Sift the flour, baking powder, cinnamon, and salt into a bowl.

2. Beat the butter, sugar, and vanilla in a bowl until pale and creamy. Add the eggs one at a time, beating until just blended after each addition. Gradually beat in the flour mixture, alternating with the cream. Stir in the strawberries. Spoon the batter into the paper liners, filling each one two-thirds full.

3. Bake for 20–25 minutes, until golden brown and a toothpick inserted into the centers comes out clean. Transfer the muffin pan to a wire rack. Let cool completely before removing the cupcakes.

FROSTING 4. Combine the egg whites and sugar in a double boiler over barely simmering water. Whisk until the mixture reaches 160°F (80°C) and the sugar has dissolved.

5. Remove from the heat and whisk until stiff peaks form and the mixture has cooled to room temperature. Add the butter, 2 tablespoons at a time, adding more once each addition has been incorporated. If the frosting looks curdled, continue to beat until thick and smooth again.

6. Fill a pastry (piping) bag with the frosting. Pipe a rosette on each cupcake, and top with a strawberry. Let set for 15 minutes before serving.

• **IF YOU LIKED THIS RECIPE, TRY THE STRAWBERRY DELIGHT CUPCAKES ON PAGE 114.**

BULL'S EYE CUPCAKES

CUPCAKES 1⅓ cups (200 g) all-purpose (plain) flour • 1½ teaspoons baking powder • ⅛ teaspoon salt • ½ cup (120 g) unsalted butter, softened • 1 cup (200 g) sugar • 1 teaspoon vanilla extract (essence) • 2 large eggs • ½ cup (120 ml) milk • 12 candied (glacé) cherries

FROSTING 2 cups (300 g) confectioners' (icing) sugar • 1–2 tablespoons boiling water • 1 tube black frosting (icing) • 1 tube red frosting (icing)

MAKES 12 CUPCAKES • **PREPARATION** 30 MINUTES • **BAKING** 20–25 MINUTES

CUPCAKES 1. Preheat the oven to 325°F (170°C/gas 3). Line a 12-cup muffin pan with paper liners. Sift the flour, baking powder, and salt into a bowl. **2.** Beat the butter, sugar, and vanilla in a bowl until pale and creamy. Add the eggs one at a time, beating until just blended after each addition. Beat in the flour mixture, alternating with the milk.

3. Spoon half of the batter into the paper liners. Place a cherry in the center of each one and cover with the remaining batter. **4.** Bake for 20–25 minutes, until golden brown and a toothpick inserted into the centers comes out clean. Transfer the muffin pan to a wire rack. Let cool completely before removing the cupcakes.

FROSTING 5. Combine the confectioners' sugar with enough of the water in a small bowl to make a smooth frosting. Spread over the cupcakes. Add a tip to the tube of black frosting and pipe three circles on the three circles on six of the cupcakes. Add a tip to the tube of red frosting and pipe three circles on the remaining six cupcakes. Fill in the central circles with black or red frosting.

• **IF YOU LIKED THIS RECIPE, TRY THE NEENISH CUPCAKES ON PAGE 106.**

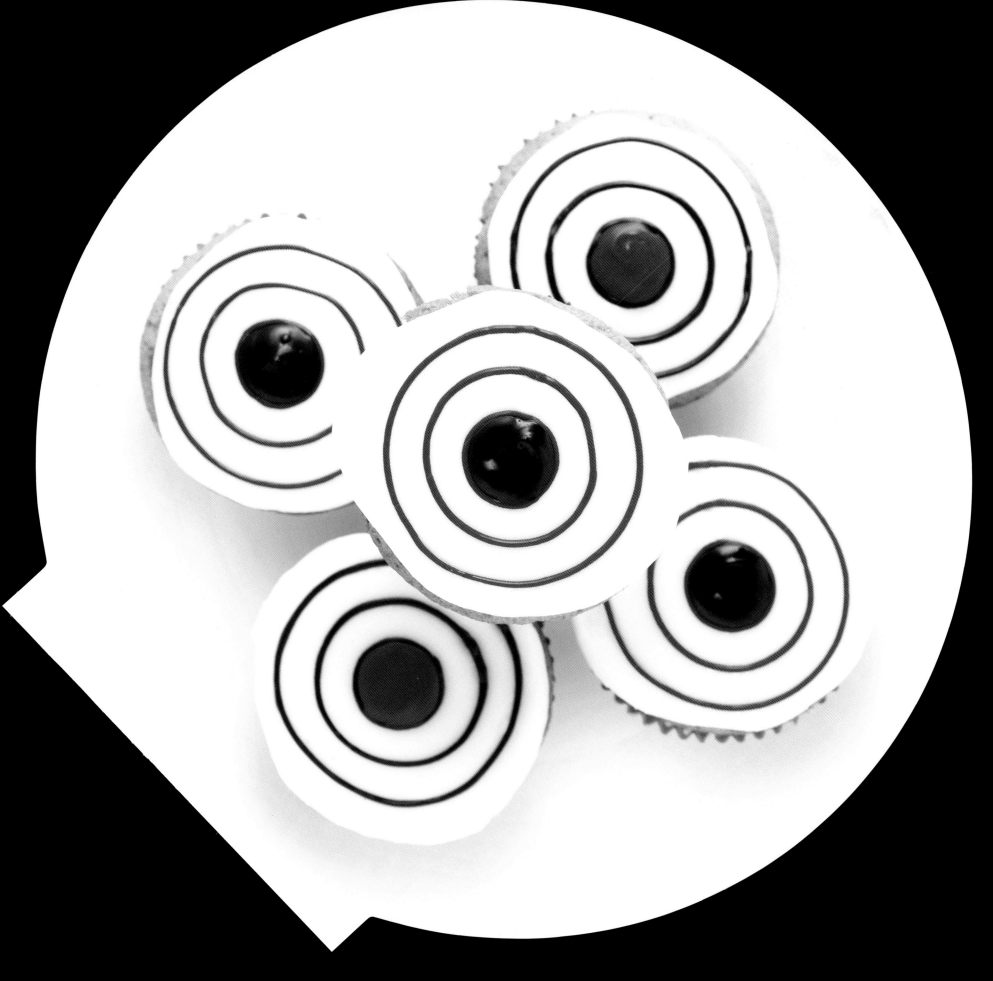

WHITE CHOCOLATE BLUEBERRY CUPCAKES

CUPCAKES 3 ounces (90 g) white chocolate, coarsely chopped • ⅓ cup (90 ml) light (single) cream • 1 cup (150 g) all-purpose (plain) flour • 1 teaspoon baking powder • ½ teaspoon ground cinnamon • ⅛ teaspoon salt • ⅓ cup (90 g) unsalted butter, softened • 1 cup (200 g) sugar • 1 teaspoon vanilla extract (essence) • 2 large eggs 1 cup (150 g) blueberries + 12 extra, to decorate

WHITE CHOCOLATE FROSTING 4 ounces (120 g) white chocolate, coarsely chopped • ½ cup (120 ml) light (single) cream • 4 tablespoons confectioners' (icing) sugar • Colored cachous (balls), to decorate

MAKES 12 CUPCAKES • **PREPARATION** 30 MINUTES + 10 MINUTES TO CHILL • **BAKING** 25–30 MINUTES

CUPCAKES 1. Preheat the oven to 325°F (170°C/gas 3). Line a 12-cup muffin pan with paper liners.

2. Melt the chocolate and cream in a double boiler over barely simmering water, stirring until smooth. Remove from the heat and let cool. Sift the flour, baking powder, cinnamon, and salt into a small bowl.

3. Beat the butter, sugar, and vanilla in a bowl until pale and creamy. Add the eggs one at a time, beating until just blended after each addition. Gradually beat in the flour mixture and melted chocolate. Stir in the blueberries. Spoon the batter into the paper liners, filling each one two-thirds full.

4. Bake for 25–30 minutes, until golden brown and a toothpick inserted into the centers comes out clean. Transfer the muffin pan to a wire rack. Let cool completely before removing the cupcakes.

WHITE CHOCOLATE FROSTING 5. Melt the chocolate and cream in a double boiler over barely simmering water, stirring until smooth. Remove from the heat and stir in the confectioners' sugar. Chill until thickened, about 10 minutes.

6. Spread the frosting over the cupcakes. Top each one with a blueberry and some colored cachous.

• IF YOU LIKED THIS RECIPE, TRY THE BLUEBERRY CUPCAKES ON PAGE 10.

CUPCAKES 3½ ounces (100 g) dark chocolate, chopped • ⅓ cup (90 ml) light (single) cream 1 cup (150 g) all-purpose (plain) flour • 2 tablespoons unsweetened cocoa powder • 1 teaspoon baking powder • ⅛ teaspoon salt • ⅓ cup (90 g) unsalted butter, softened • 1 cup (200 g) sugar • 1 teaspoon vanilla extract (essence) • 2 large eggs
CHOCOLATE BUTTERCREAM 3½ ounces (100 g) milk chocolate, chopped • ½ cup (120 g) unsalted butter, softened • ¼ teaspoon vanilla extract (essence) • ½ tablespoon milk • ½ cup (75 g) confectioners' (icing) sugar • 12 pink candy roses, to decorate

MAKES 12 CUPCAKES • **PREPARATION** 45 MINUTES • **BAKING** 25–30 MINUTES

CHOCOLATE ROSE CUPCAKES

CUPCAKES 1. Preheat the oven to 325°F (170°C/gas 3). Line a 12-cup muffin pan with paper liners. Line a baking sheet with parchment paper.

2. Melt the chocolate and cream in a double boiler over barely simmering water, stirring until smooth. Set aside to cool. Sift the flour, cocoa, baking powder, and salt into a bowl.

3. Beat the butter, sugar, and vanilla in a bowl until pale and creamy. Add the eggs one at a time, beating until just blended after each addition. Gradually beat in the flour mixture and chocolate. Spoon the batter into the paper liners, filling each one two-thirds full.

4. Bake for 25–30 minutes, until a toothpick inserted into the centers comes out clean. Transfer the muffin pan to a wire rack. Let cool completely before removing the cupcakes.

CHOCOLATE BUTTERCREAM 5. Melt the chocolate in a double boiler over barely simmering water, or in the microwave. Set aside to cool.

6. Beat the butter and vanilla in a bowl until pale and creamy. Pour in the milk and chocolate, beating until blended. Gradually beat in the confectioners' sugar.

7. Spoon the buttercream into a pastry (piping) bag fitted with a star-shaped nozzle and pipe onto the cupcakes. Top each one with a candy rose.

IF YOU LIKED THIS RECIPE, TRY THE ROSY CUPCAKES ON PAGE 18.

LEMON MERINGUE CUPCAKES

CUPCAKES 3 cups (450 g) all-purpose (...n) flour • 1 tablespoon baking powder • ½ teaspoon salt ...p (250 g) butter, softened • 2 cups (400 g) sugar • 4 large eggs ...y grated zest of 3 unwaxed lemons (about 3 tablespoons) • 2 tablespoons ...queezed lemon juice • 1 teaspoon vanilla extract (essence) • 1 cup (250 ml) buttermilk

1 cup (250 ml) lemon curd

...UE FROSTING ¾ cup (150 g) + 2 tablespoons sugar • ⅓ cup (90 ml) water • 1 tablespoon light corn (golden) syrup • 3 large egg whites • Yellow sugar, to decorate

MAKES 20–24 CUPCAKES • **PREPARATION** 45 MINUTES + 15 MINUTES TO COOL • **BAKING** 20–25 MINUTES

CUPCAKES 1. Preheat the oven to 325°F (170°C/gas 3). Line two 12-cup muffin pans with paper liners. Sift the flour, baking powder, and salt into a bowl.

2. Beat the butter and sugar in a bowl until pale and creamy. Add the eggs one at a time, beating until just combined after each addition. Gradually beat in the lemon zest and juice, vanilla, flour mixture, and buttermilk. Spoon the batter into the paper liners, filling each one two-thirds full.

3. Bake for 20–25 minutes, until golden brown. Transfer the muffin pans to a wire rack. Let cool completely before removing the cupcakes.

MERINGUE FROSTING 4. Combine ¾ cup (150 g) of sugar with the water and corn syrup in a small saucepan. Bring to a boil

over medium heat, stirring occasionally, until the sugar dissolves. Simmer, without stirring, until the syrup reaches the soft ball stage (about 240°F /120°C). Remove from the heat.

5. Beat the egg whites until soft peaks form. Add the remaining 2 tablespoons of sugar, beating to combine. Add the corn syrup mixture to the egg white mixture in a slow, steady stream. Beat until completely cool and stiff peaks form, 5–7 minutes.

6. Spread 1 tablespoon of lemon curd on each cupcake. Fill a pastry (piping) bag fitted with a star tip with frosting. Pipe onto each cupcake, swirling up to form a peak. Sprinkle with yellow sugar. Brown with a kitchen blow torch. Let cool for 15 minutes before serving.

IF YOU LIKED THIS RECIPE, TRY THE IRISH COFFEE CUPCAKES ON PAGE 110.

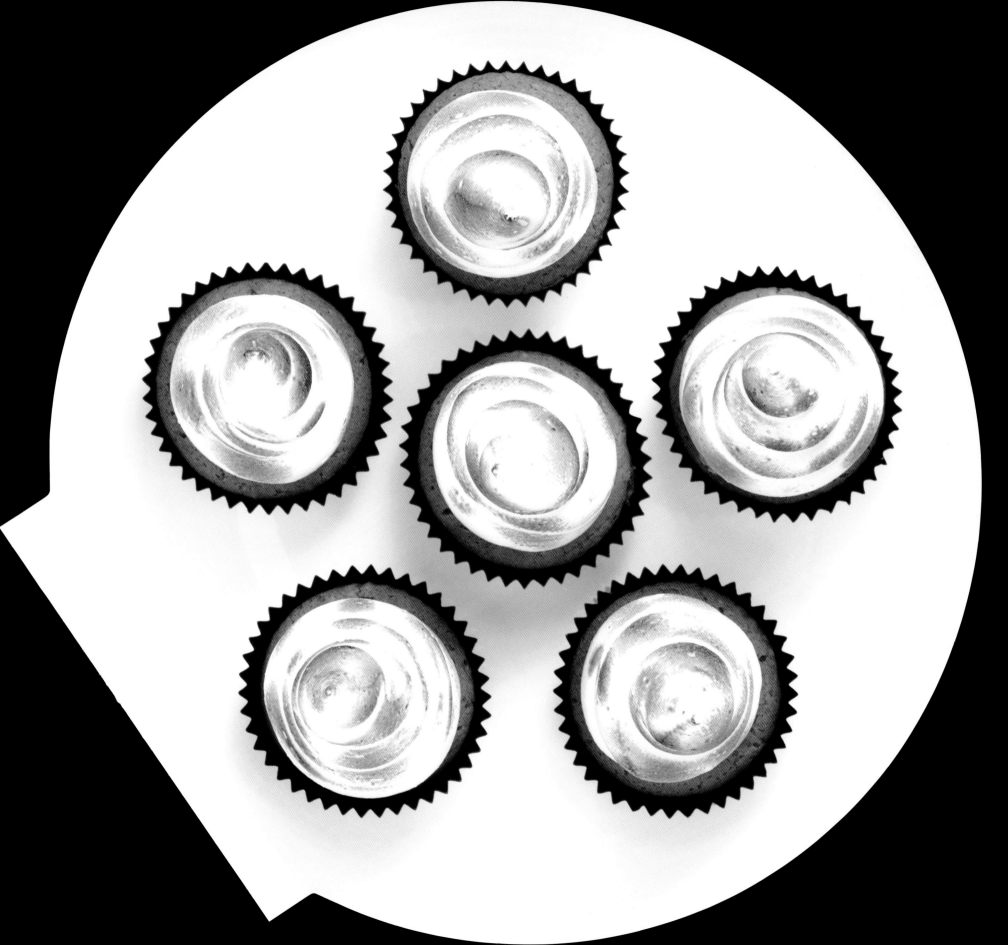

NEENISH CUPCAKES

CUPCAKES 1⅓ cups (200 g) all-purpose (plain) flour • 1½ teaspoons baking powder • 1 teaspoon ground cinnamon • ⅛ teaspoon salt • ⅓ cup (30 g) finely ground almonds • 1 cup (200 g) sugar • 2 large eggs • 1 teaspoon vanilla extract (essence) • 1 cup (250 ml) light (single) cream • ½ cup (150 g) raspberry preserves (jam)

FROSTING 2 cups (300 g) confectioners' (icing) sugar • 2-3 tablespoons milk 2 tablespoons unsweetened cocoa powder

MAKES 12 CUPCAKES • PREPARATION 30 MINUTES + 30 MINUTES TO SET • BAKING 20-25 MINUTES

CUPCAKES 1. Preheat the oven to 325°F (170°C/gas 3). Line a 12-cup muffin pan with paper liners. Sift the flour, baking powder, cinnamon, and salt into a bowl. Stir in the almonds.

2. Beat the sugar, eggs, and vanilla in a bowl until pale and thick. Gradually beat in the flour mixture and cream. Spoon the batter into the prepared cups, filling each one two-thirds full.

3. Bake for 20-25 minutes, until golden brown and a toothpick inserted into the centers comes out clean. Transfer the muffin pan to a wire rack. Let cool completely before removing the cupcakes.

4. Spread a teaspoon of raspberry preserves on each cupcake.

FROSTING 5. Combine the confectioners' sugar and milk in a small bowl. Divide evenly between two small bowls and stir the cocoa into one.

6. Spread the white frosting over half of each cupcake and the chocolate frosting over the other half, making a clearcut line down the center. Let set for 30 minutes before serving.

• IF YOU LIKED THIS RECIPE, TRY THE MARS BAR CUPCAKES ON PAGE 56.

CHOCOLATE CANDY CUPCAKES

CUPCAKES 1 cup (150 g) all-purpose (plain) flour • ¼ cup (30 g) unsweetened cocoa powder • 1 teaspoon baking powder • ¼ teaspoon baking soda (bicarbonate of soda) • ½ cup (100 g) firmly packed dark brown sugar • ⅓ cup (90 g) salted butter, softened 1 teaspoon vanilla extract (essence) • 1 large egg • ¼ cup (60 ml) milk yellow, red, and green food coloring • Candy-coated chocolates (M&M's or Smarties), to decorate **FROSTING** 2 cups (300 g) confectioners' (icing) sugar • 1–2 tablespoons boiling water • Few drops each

MAKES 12 CUPCAKES • **PREPARATION** 30 MINUTES • **BAKING** 20–25 MINUTES

CUPCAKES 1. Preheat the oven to 325°F (170°C/gas 3). Line a 12-cup muffin pan with paper liners. Sift the flour, cocoa, baking powder, and baking soda into a bowl.

2. Beat the brown sugar, butter, and vanilla in a bowl until creamy. Add the egg, beating until just combined. Gradually beat in the flour mixture, alternating with the milk. Spoon the batter into the prepared cups, filling each one two-thirds full.

3. Bake for 20–25 minutes, until golden brown and a toothpick inserted into the centers comes out

clean. Transfer the muffin pan to a wire rack. Let cool completely before removing the cupcakes.

FROSTING 4. Mix the confectioners' sugar with enough of the water in a small bowl to make a smooth frosting. Divide the frosting evenly among three small bowls. Add a few drops of food coloring to each bowl to make bright yellow, red, and green frostings.

5. Spread the frostings over the cupcakes, making four of each color. Decorate with candy-coated chocolates.

● **IF YOU LIKED THIS RECIPE, TRY THE JELLY BEAN CUPCAKES ON PAGE 44.**

IRISH COFFEE CUPCAKES

CUPCAKES 1¼ cups (180 g) all-purpose (plain) flour • 1 teaspoon baking powder • ⅛ teaspoon salt • 1 tablespoon instant coffee granules • 1 tablespoon boiling water • ⅔ cup (150 g) unsalted butter, softened • ¾ cup (150 g) firmly packed light brown sugar • 3 large eggs • ½ teaspoon vanilla extract (essence) • ½ cup (75 g)

DECORATION 1 pound (500 g) white fondant • 1 tablespoon coffee liqueur • ½ cup (150 g) orange marmalade, warmed and strained • Sugar or candy four-leaf clovers and buckles and belts, to decorate confectioners' (icing) sugar

MAKES 12 CUPCAKES • PREPARATION 45 MINUTES • BAKING 20–25 MINUTES

CUPCAKES 1. Preheat the oven to 350°F (180°C/gas 4). Line a 12-cup muffin pan with paper liners. Sift the flour, baking powder, and salt into a bowl. Dissolve the coffee granules in the boiling water in a cup.

2. Beat the butter and brown sugar in a bowl until creamy. Add the eggs one at a time, beating until just combined after each addition. Beat in the flour mixture, coffee mixture, and vanilla. Spoon the batter into the paper liners, filling each one two-thirds full.

3. Bake for 20–25 minutes, until a toothpick inserted into the centers comes out clean. Transfer the muffin pan to a wire rack. Let cool completely before removing the cupcakes.

DECORATION 4. Knead the fondant until soft and pliable. Use a toothpick dipped in the coffee liqueur to dab holes in the fondant. Knead until absorbed and evenly colored and flavored.

5. Dust a work surface with confectioners' sugar. Roll out the fondant to ⅛ inch (3 mm) thick. Use a small sharp knife to cut out rounds large enough to cover the entire cupcakes.

6. Remove the paper liners from the cupcakes and brush all over with marmalade. Place the fondant rounds on top. Smooth over the sides and trim at the bases to fit. Decorate with the four-leaf clovers and buckles and belts.

IF YOU LIKED THIS RECIPE, TRY THE MINT CHOCOLATE CUPCAKES ON PAGE 64.

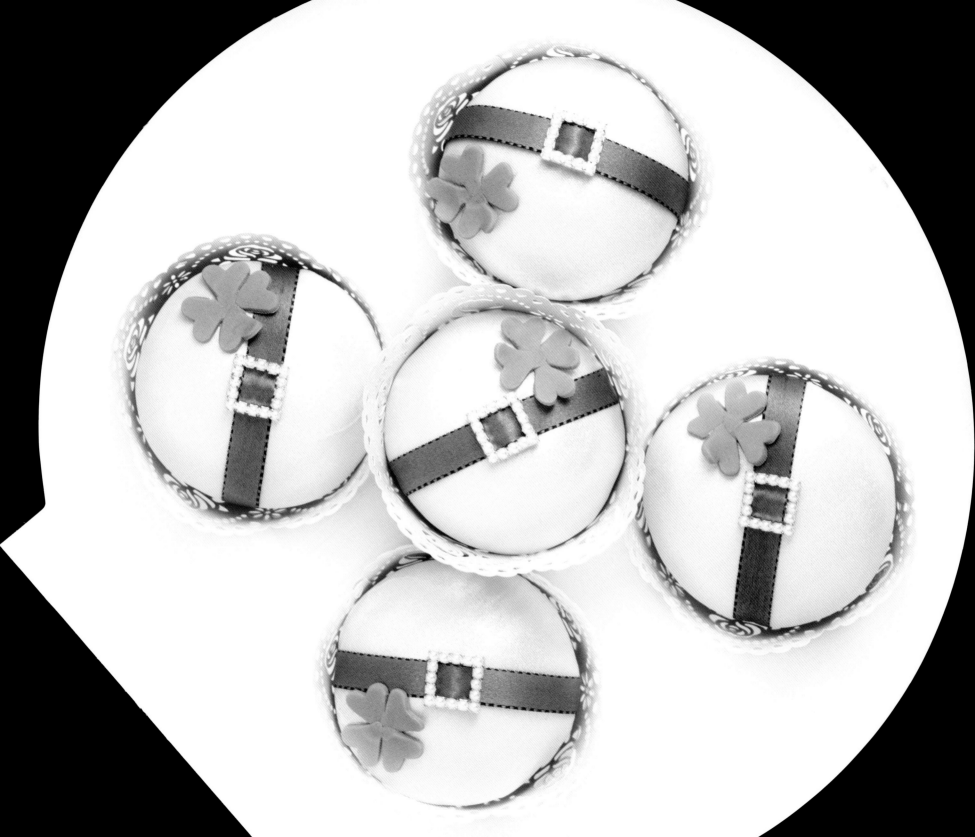

GLUTEN-FREE CUPCAKES

CUPCAKES ½ cup (60 g) amaranth flour • ¾ cup (120 g) rice flour • 1 teaspoon baking soda (bicarbonate of soda) • ⅛ teaspoon salt • 1 teaspoon ground cinnamon • ¼ teaspoon ground cloves • ¾ cup (150 g) sugar • ½ cup (120 ml) vegetable oil • ¼ cup (60 ml) water • 2 large eggs • 1 tart apple, such as Granny Smith, peeled, cored, and grated • ½ cup (60 g) xanthan gum • ¾ cup (135 g) **CREAM CHEESE FROSTING** 1 cup (250 g) cream cheese, softened • 1 cup (150 g) confectioners' (icing) sugar • 1 tablespoon freshly squeezed lemon juice • Few drops each pink and yellow food coloring • Candy flowers, to decorate • Silver cachous (balls), to decorate

MAKES 12 CUPCAKES • **PREPARATION** 45 MINUTES • **BAKING** 20–25 MINUTES

CUPCAKES 1. Preheat the oven to 325°F (170°C/ gas 3). Line a 12-cup muffin pan with paper liners. Sift both flours, the baking soda, cinnamon, cloves, and salt into a bowl. Add the xanthan gum.

2. Beat the eggs in a bowl until frothy. Add the sugar, oil, and water and beat until incorporated. Gradually beat in the flour mixture. Stir in the apple and walnuts. Spoon the batter into the paper liners, filling each one two-thirds full.

3. Bake for 25–30 minutes, until golden brown and a toothpick inserted into the centers comes out clean. Transfer the muffin pan to a wire rack. Let cool completely before removing the cupcakes.

CREAM CHEESE FROSTING 4. Beat the cream cheese until smooth. Add the confectioners' sugar and lemon juice, beating until just combined.

5. Divide the frosting evenly between two bowls and stir a few drops of pink food coloring into one bowl and a few drops of yellow food coloring into the other.

6. Spread the yellow frosting on half of the cupcakes and the pink frosting on the other half. Decorate each cupcake differently, using different combinations of candy flowers and silver cachous.

● **IF YOU LIKED THIS RECIPE, TRY THE MERINGUE CUPCAKES ON PAGE 28.**

STRAWBERRY DELIGHT CUPCAKES

CUPCAKES 1½ cups (225 g) self-rising flour • ⅛ teaspoon salt • ½ cup (120 g) unsalted butter, softened • ¾ cup (150 g) sugar • ½ teaspoon vanilla extract (essence) • 2 large eggs • ½ cup (120 ml) milk • 1 tablespoon strawberry liqueur

STRAWBERRY CREAM 1 cup (250 ml) heavy (double) cream • 2 tablespoons confectioners' (icing) sugar + extra, to dust • 1 tablespoon strawberry liqueur • ½ teaspoon vanilla extract (essence) • 10-12 fresh strawberries, sliced

MAKES 12 CUPCAKES • **PREPARATION** 30 MINUTES • **BAKING** 25-30 MINUTES

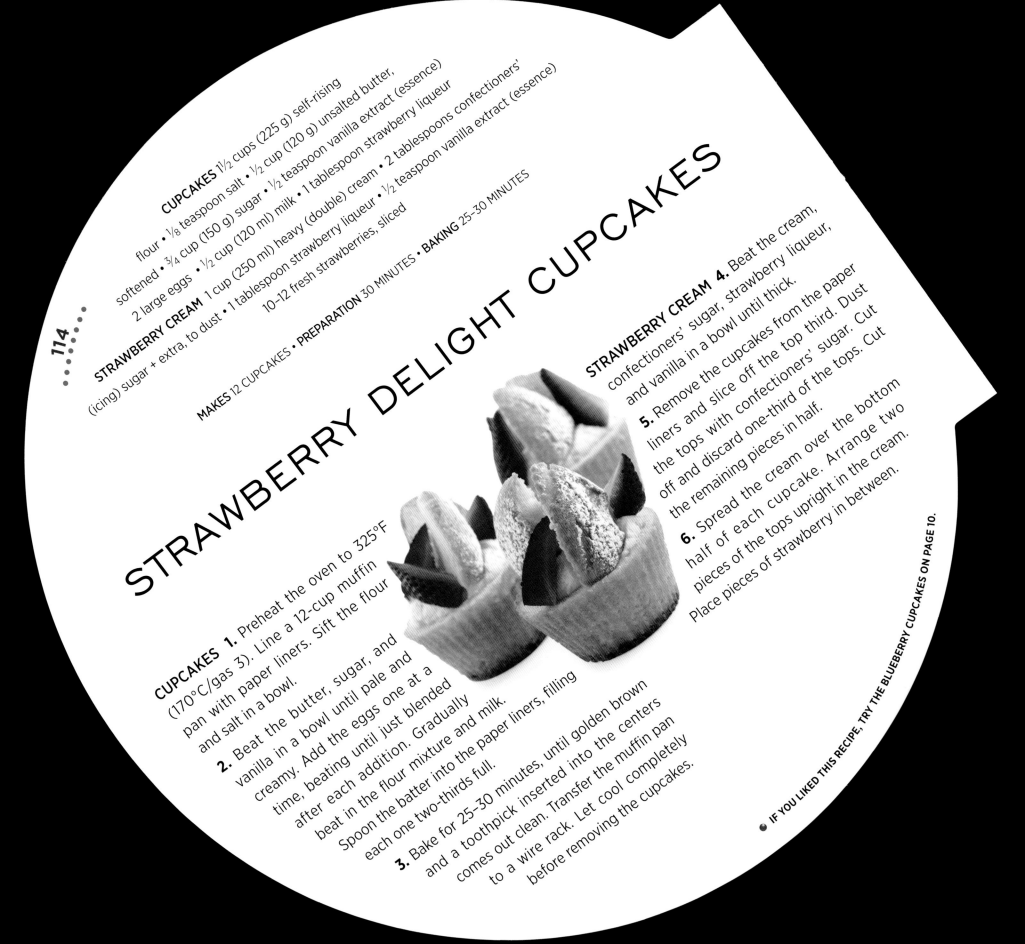

CUPCAKES 1. Preheat the oven to 325°F (170°C/gas 3). Line a 12-cup muffin pan with paper liners. Sift the flour and salt in a bowl.

2. Beat the butter, sugar, and vanilla in a bowl until pale and creamy. Add the eggs one at a time, beating until just blended after each addition. Gradually beat in the flour mixture and milk. Spoon the batter into the paper liners, filling each one two-thirds full.

3. Bake for 25-30 minutes, until golden brown and a toothpick inserted into the centers comes out clean. Transfer the muffin pan to a wire rack. Let cool completely before removing the cupcakes.

STRAWBERRY CREAM 4. Beat the cream, confectioners' sugar, strawberry liqueur, and vanilla in a bowl until thick.

5. Remove the cupcakes from the paper liners and slice off the top third. Dust the tops with confectioners' sugar. Cut off and discard one-third of the tops. Cut the remaining pieces in half.

6. Spread the cream over the bottom half of each cupcake. Arrange two pieces of the tops upright in the cream. Place pieces of strawberry in between.

● **IF YOU LIKED THIS RECIPE, TRY THE BLUEBERRY CUPCAKES ON PAGE 10.**

CHOCOLATE BUTTERFLY CAKES

CUPCAKES 1⅓ cups (200 g) all-purpose (plain) flour • ⅔ cup (100 g) unsweetened cocoa powder • 2 teaspoons baking powder • ¼ teaspoon salt • ⅔ cup (150 g) unsalted butter, softened 1 cup (200 g) sugar • 2 large eggs • ½ cup (120 ml) milk • 1 tablespoon orange liqueur

TOPPING ½ cup (120 g) unsalted butter, softened • 2 cups (300 g) confectioners' (icing) sugar + extra, to dust • 1 teaspoon vanilla extract (essence) • Few drops each yellow and pink food coloring • Yellow candy, for eyes • Liquorice lace, for feelers • Red candy, for nose

MAKES 12 CUPCAKES • **PREPARATION** 45 MINUTES + 30 MINUTES TO SET • **BAKING** 20–25 MINUTES

CUPCAKES **1.** Preheat the oven to 350°F (180°C/gas 4). Line a 12-cup muffin pan with paper liners. Sift the flour, cocoa, baking powder, and salt into a bowl.

2. Beat the butter and sugar in a bowl until pale and creamy. Add the eggs one at a time, beating until just blended after each addition. Gradually beat in the flour mixture, alternating with the milk and orange liqueur. Spoon the batter into the paper liners, filling each one two-thirds full.

3. Bake for 20–25 minutes, until a toothpick inserted into the centers comes out clean. Transfer the muffin pan to a wire rack. Let cool completely before removing the cupcakes.

TOPPING **4.** Beat the butter and confectioners' sugar in a bowl until creamy. Stir in the water and vanilla. Put a quarter of the frosting in a small bowl and color with pink food coloring. Color the remaining frosting yellow.

5. Cut the rounded top off each cupcake. Dust the tops with confectioners' sugar, then cut in half to make two "wings."

6. Spread the cupcakes with yellow frosting. Arrange a pair of "wings" on each cupcake. Add yellow candy for eyes, licorice to make feelers, and red candy for the nose. Put the pink frosting in a pastry (piping) bag and pipe dots of frosting between the wings. Let set for 30 minutes before serving.

● **IF YOU LIKED THIS RECIPE, TRY THE BUTTERFLY CUPCAKES ON PAGE 12.**

CHOCOLATE PEAR CUPCAKES

MAKES 10 CUPCAKES • **PREPARATION** 45 MINUTES + 15 MINUTES TO COOL • **BAKING** 20–25 MINUTES

10 small pears, peeled, stalks intact • 3 cups (750 ml) water • 2 teaspoons vanilla bean paste • 1½ cups (300 g) superfine (caster) sugar • 2 tablespoons unsweetened cocoa powder + ¼ cup (30 g) extra • 7 ounces (200 g) dark chocolate, coarsely chopped • ¾ cup (180 g) salted butter, melted • 1⅓ cups (200 g) all-purpose (plain) flour • 1 teaspoon baking powder • 2 large eggs, lightly beaten

1. Preheat the oven to 350°F (180°C/gas 4). Line ten muffin cups with paper or foil liners. Use a melon baller to scoop out the base and core from each pear.

2. Combine the water, vanilla bean paste, and half the sugar in a medium saucepan over low heat. Cook and stir until the sugar dissolves, about 5 minutes. Bring to a boil. Add the pears and simmer, turning occasionally, until tender, about 10 minutes. Use a slotted spoon to transfer the pears to a plate to drain. Whisk the 2 tablespoons of cocoa into the syrup. Simmer until the syrup thickens slightly, 10–15 minutes.

3. Melt the chocolate and butter in a double boiler over barely simmering water, stirring until smooth. Remove from the heat. Sift in the flour and baking powder. Add the eggs, extra cocoa, and remaining sugar and stir until well combined.

4. Spoon the batter into the prepared pans. Gently press a pear into the center of each cupcake.

5. Bake for 20–25 minutes, until a toothpick inserted into the centers comes out clean. Set aside for 15 minutes to cool. Carefully remove from the pans and divide among serving plates. Drizzle with the chocolate syrup and serve warm.

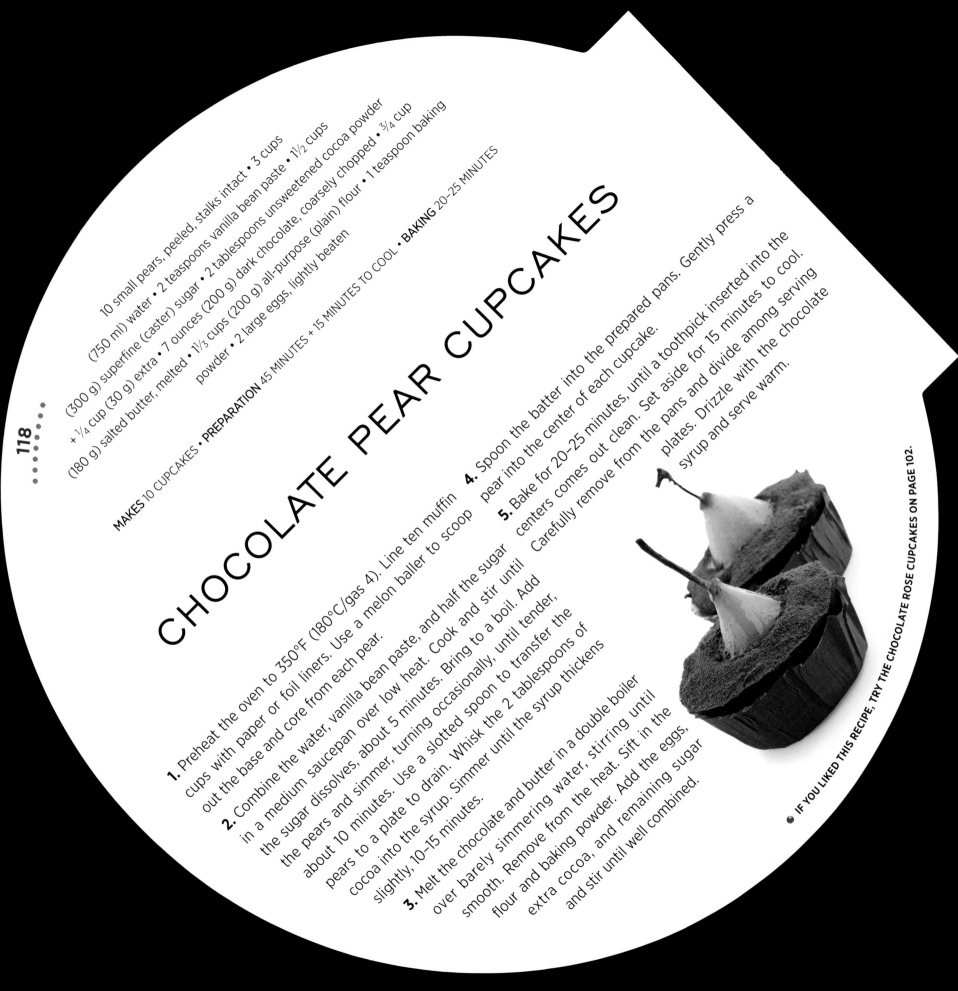

• **IF YOU LIKED THIS RECIPE, TRY THE CHOCOLATE ROSE CUPCAKES ON PAGE 102.**

BEETLE CUPCAKES

CUPCAKES ½ cup (75 g) all-purpose (plain) flour • ½ cup (75 g) self-rising flour • ⅓ cup (50 g) unsweetened cocoa powder • ¼ teaspoon baking soda (bicarbonate of soda) • ⅛ teaspoon salt • ⅓ cup (90 g) unsalted butter, softened • ½ cup (100 g) firmly packed dark brown sugar • 1 large egg • 1 teaspoon vanilla extract (essence) • ¼ cup (60 ml) milk

DECORATION 2 cups (300 g) confectioners' (icing) sugar • 3 ounces (90 g) red fondant • 2 ounces (60 g) dark chocolate, melted and cooled • Few drops each light and dark green food coloring

MAKES 12 CUPCAKES • **PREPARATION** 45 MINUTES • **BAKING** 20–25 MINUTES

CUPCAKES 1. Preheat the oven to 350°F (180°C/gas 4). Line a 12-cup muffin pan with paper liners. Sift both flours, the cocoa, baking soda, and salt into a bowl.
2. Beat the butter, brown sugar, egg, and vanilla in a bowl until creamy. Gradually beat in the flour mixture and milk. Spoon the batter into the paper liners, filling each one two-thirds full.
3. Bake for 20–25 minutes, until a toothpick inserted into the centers comes out clean. Transfer the muffin pan to a wire rack. Let cool completely before removing the cupcakes.

DECORATION 4. Mix the confectioners' sugar and water in a bowl, stirring until smooth. Put a quarter of the frosting in a small bowl and color dark green. Color the remaining frosting with the light green coloring.
5. Spread the light green frosting over the cupcakes. Put the dark green frosting in a small plastic food bag and snip off one corner. Pipe over the cupcakes.
6. Break the red fondant into 12 pieces and form into beetle shapes. Shape the cooled chocolate into heads and press into the red fondant.

● **IF YOU LIKED THIS RECIPE, TRY THE FUNNY FACE CUPCAKES ON PAGE 124.**

butter • 2 ounces (60 g) dark chocolate, chopped • ½ cup (75 g) unsweetened cocoa powder • ¾ cup (120 g) all-purpose (plain) flour • ½ teaspoon baking soda (bicarbonate of soda) • 1 teaspoon baking powder 2 large eggs • ¾ cup (150 g) sugar • 1 teaspoon vanilla extract (essence) • ½ teaspoon salt ½ cup (120 ml) sour cream

PEANUT BUTTER FROSTING ⅓ cup (90 ml) heavy (double) cream • 1 cup (150 g) confectioners' (icing) sugar • ¾ cup (180 g) creamy peanut butter • 5 tablespoons unsalted butter, softened • ½ teaspoon vanilla extract

TOFFEE 2 cups (400 g) sugar • ¾ cup (180 ml) water • ½ cup (60 g) salted peanuts

MAKES 12 CUPCAKES • PREPARATION 1 HOUR • BAKING 20–25 MINUTES

SALTED PEANUT CUPCAKES

CUPCAKES 1. Preheat the oven to 350°F (180°C/gas 4). Put the butter, chocolate, and cocoa in a double boiler over barely simmering water, stirring until smooth. Set aside to cool a little.

2. Sift the flour, baking soda, and baking powder into a bowl.

3. Beat the eggs in a bowl until frothy. Add the sugar, vanilla, and salt and beat until well combined. Beat in the chocolate mixture, followed by the flour and sour cream. Spoon the batter into the paper liners, filling each one two-thirds full.

4. Bake for 20–25 minutes, until a toothpick inserted into the centers comes out clean. Transfer the muffin pan to a wire rack. Let cool completely before removing the cupcakes.

PEANUT BUTTER FROSTING 5. Beat the cream until soft peaks form. Set aside. Beat the confectioners' sugar, peanut butter, butter, and vanilla in a bowl until creamy. Fold in the cream.

6. Put the frosting in a pastry (piping) bag and pipe over the cupcakes.

TOFFEE 7. Bring the sugar and water to a boil in a small saucepan over medium heat. Spread the peanuts in a baking pan and pour the toffee over the top. Let harden, then break into shards. Decorate the cupcakes with the shards of peanut toffee.

CARAMEL CUPCAKES ON PAGE 68.

FUNNY FACE CUPCAKES

MAKES 12 CUPCAKES • PREPARATION 45 MINUTES • **BAKING** 20–25 MINUTES

CUPCAKES ¾ cup (120 g) all-purpose (plain) flour • 3 tablespoons unsweetened cocoa powder (plain) baking powder • ⅛ teaspoon salt • ½ cup (120 g) unsalted butter, softened ¾ cup (150 g) firmly packed dark brown sugar • 3½ ounces (100 g) marshmallows, chopped 2 large eggs • 3 tablespoons milk • ½ teaspoon vanilla extract (essence)

DECORATION 8 ounces (250 g) red fondant • 2 multipacks (mixed colors) fondant ½ cup (150 g) orange marmalade, warmed and strained • Black candy writer, for eyes

CUPCAKES 1. Preheat the oven to 350°F (180°C/gas 4). Line a 12-cup muffin pan with paper liners. Sift the flour, cocoa, baking powder, and salt into a bowl.

2. Beat the butter, brown sugar, and vanilla in a bowl until creamy. Add the eggs one at a time, beating until just blended after each addition. Gradually beat in the flour mixture, alternating with the milk. Stir in the marsh-mallows. Spoon the batter into the paper liners, filling each one two-thirds full.

3. Bake for 20–25 minutes, until golden brown and a toothpick inserted into the centers comes out clean. Transfer the muffin pan to a wire rack. Let cool completely before removing the cupcakes.

DECORATION 4. Roll out the red fondant to ⅛ inch (3 mm) thick. Use a cookie cutter or glass to cut out rounds large enough to cover the cupcakes. Brush the cupcakes with the marmalade and stick the fondant rounds to them.

5. Roll out the different colored fondants and create funny faces. Use the black candy writer to make the eyes. Get creative and have fun!

● IF YOU LIKED THIS RECIPE, TRY THE PIRATE CUPCAKES ON PAGE 50.

TABBY CAT CUPCAKES

CUPCAKES 1½ cups (225 g) all-purpose (plain) flour • 1½ teaspoons baking powder • 2 tablespoons unsweetened cocoa powder • ½ teaspoon baking powder • ½ teaspoon salt • 1 cup (200 g) sugar • 2 large eggs • 1 teaspoon vanilla extract (essence) • ½ cup (120 ml) heavy (double) cream • ½ cup (120 g) milk chocolate chips

BUTTER FROSTING ½ cup (90 g) unsalted butter, softened • ½ teaspoon orange vanilla extract (essence) 1½ cups (225 g) confectioners' (icing) sugar • ½ teaspoon orange food coloring

DECORATION 36 small, colored candy-coated buttons • Black liquorice • 1 ounce (30 g) dark chocolate, melted • Chocolate wafers

MAKES 12 CUPCAKES • PREPARATION 45 MINUTES • **BAKING** 20-25 MINUTES

CUPCAKES 1. Preheat the oven to 350°F (180°C/gas 4). Line a 12-cup muffin pan with paper liners. Sift the flour, cocoa, baking powder, and salt into a bowl.
2. Beat the sugar, eggs, and vanilla in a bowl until pale and thick. Add the flour mixture, alternating with the cream. Stir in the chocolate chips. Spoon the batter into the paper liners, filling each one two-thirds full.
3. Bake for 20-25 minutes, until golden brown and a toothpick inserted into the centers comes out clean. Transfer the muffin pan to a wire rack. Let cool completely before removing the cupcakes.

BUTTER FROSTING 4. Beat the butter and vanilla in a small bowl until combined. Gradually add the confectioners' sugar, beating until creamy. Divide the frosting evenly between two small bowls. Tint one bowl with orange food coloring.

DECORATION 5. Roughly spread the two frostings on the cupcakes to create mottled tabby cat-type markings. Create cat faces using candy-coated buttons for the eyes and mouths. Slice thin strips of black liquorice and use for tails. Put the melted chocolate into a small plastic food bag and snip off one corner. Drizzle between the eyes and mouths to make the whiskers. Cut the chocolate wafers into small triangles and position as ears.

● IF YOU LIKED THIS RECIPE, TRY THE BEETLE CUPCAKES ON PAGE 120.

INDEX